Awards and Accolades
for *Teaching Kids to Love the Earth*

Benjamin Franklin Award • Best Parenting/Child Care Book

Midwest Independent Publishers Association • Best Environmental Book

Translated into Portuguese and featured athe the
International Earth Summit in Rio de Janeiro

"Forget the reference to kids in the title—this book is for people of all ages to rediscover the outdoors. Read it, grab a friend, and head out . . . *Teaching Kids to Love the Earth* encourages adults to experience nature not by sitting on a rock as a bystander, but by taking 'a free-flight romp through a city park.'"

—**Oregonian**

"This idea book for adults uses simple, quiet anecdotes . . . to set the tone for activities designed to inspire nature discovery and exploration. Chock-full of ideas . . . this attractive book serves as a gentle but firm reminder of the preciousness of the earth; it should be a valuable resource for teachers, parents, and others who want to instill such Earth awareness in children."

—**Booklist**

"The focus is on feeling and doing, slogging through sloughs and howling at the full moon, instead of reflective reading or sitting back and quietly observing nature . . . Although the book was written with the Northwoods environment in mind, the activities can easily be adapted to any locale."

—**The Country Today**

"Parents, grandparents, aunts, uncles, teachers, scout leaders—anyone who spends time oudoors with young people will treasure this book. It's filled with joy, hope, and love—a book to celebrate in this, the environmental decade."

—**Laura Erickson, Audubon Society**

Published by the University of Minnesota Press
111 Third Avenue South, Suite 290
Minneapolis, MN 55401-2520
http://www.upress.umn.edu

A Cataloging-in-Publication record for this book is available from the Library of Congress.

ISBN 0-8166-4197-8 (PB)

Printed in the United States of America on acid-free paper

The University of Minnesota is an equal-opportunity educator and employer.

13 12 11 10 09 08 07 06 05 04 03 02   10 9 8 7 6 5 4 3 2 1

Teaching Kids to Love the Earth

Marina Lachecki
Joseph F. Passineau
Ann Linnea
Paul Treuer

Illustrations by Carolyn Olson

University of Minnesota Press
Minneapolis · London

AN INVITATION

For the past seven years we have taught family-based nature workshops in northern Minnesota and Wisconsin. At the heart of our teaching is an idea from Rachel Carson's book, *The Sense of Wonder*. She wrote that it is more important to begin with feelings about the natural world than knowledge of it.

Inspired by Carson, we have developed a philosophy and a style of teaching that is designed to help keep alive an inborn sense of wonder about the natural world.

This book is a collection of earth-caring activities from our teaching. The activities are arranged and presented in theme sections to illustrate what we call "The Sense of Wonder Circle."

Experiences along the circle will awaken your *curiosity*, lead to *explorations* and *discoveries*, and inspire you to *share* your discoveries and sense of wonder with others. Ultimately, those experiences will lead you to care *passionately* for the earth.

Each chapter of this book contains a story to illustrate the main activity. We also have included "Did You Know," "Resources" and "Other Ideas" sections in each chapter to help you plan your own adventures. Most of our experiences were gained in our northern environment, but these activities and ideas can be tailored to fit any locale.

Use this book in a spirit of adventure. Let Carolyn Olson's art draw you into the stories and activities. To capture the essence of the activities, spend some time with what we have written. Then take your friends, your family or your students outdoors.

Finally, design and carry out activities specific to your own home and its environment. Find for yourself that sense of wonder.

This book is intended to stimulate feelings—deep feelings for the earth. These feelings may be as fragile as the gossamer wings of a damsel fly, as powerful as the love between parent and child, as stunning as an icy blast of November wind off the vast expanse of Lake Superior, or as warm as a wilderness campfire.

We hope the experiences you gain by using this book will stimulate strong feelings that will enable you and your friends to be responsible and loving caretakers of the earth.

MARINA LACHECKI
ANN LINNEA
JOSEPH F. PASSINEAU
PAUL TREUER

If a child
is to keep alive his
inborn sense of wonder,
he needs the
companionship
of at least one adult
who can share it,
rediscovering with him
the joy, excitement
and mystery of the
world we live in.

Rachel Carson

ACKNOWLEDGMENTS

Creating this book has been a team effort. During the years that we formulated the concept for this work, developed the activities, and wrote the manuscript, we were helped and supported by friends and family. We hope this brief prose adequately expresses our gratitude to all who contributed.

Our families are the heart and soul of this book. They played with us; they cried with us; they dreamed with us. They appear in the stories we've written. Many thanks to Grant, Ben and Carolyn Herman; Lyn, Forest and Dawn Passineau; Dave, Brian and Sally Schimpf; and Mary, Ramona, Galen and Eva Treuer.

We have so enjoyed meeting and playing with the families who've attended our Sense of Wonder weekends at Wolf Ridge Environmental Learning Center in Finland, Minnesota; Hawk Ridge Nature Preserve in Duluth, Minnesota; and Camp Manito-wish YMCA in Boulder Junction, Wisconsin. We thank all our workshop participants for inspiring us to teach and to share our style with others.

Steve Sorensen, Bruce Munson and Margaret Brown Olson contributed endless hours of editing and moral support. Their humor, critical insights and perspectives helped to create a more well-rounded book.

When this book was only a kernel of an idea, Mike Link, Dave Allen, Denny Olson and

Jack Pichotta encouraged us to pursue it. We thank them for believing in us. Norton Stillman added incentive when we needed it.

Turning a manuscript into a book is an arduous process. Julie Gleeson typed and retyped—and retyped. She believed in what we were sharing and reacted to our stories above and beyond the call of a typist. Hats off to Colleen Renier and Pat Greenwood who took our manuscript into its final stages.

Our deep appreciation goes to Carolyn Olson, our illustrator, who took words and created images that conveyed the joy and respect we have for the earth.

We also have a deep respect for and are grateful to Larry Fortner, Susan Gustafson and Don Tubesing who believed in the message we had to share strongly enough to publish it and who became vital members of our team.

The circle comes back to those who inspired us: grandparents and parents who took the time when we were young to hold our hands, to marvel at our discoveries, to share their excitement in being outdoors; to our children who continually provide opportunities for play; and to Rachel Carson, Sigurd Olson, Aldo Leopold and John Muir, whose commitment to the earth and beautiful words spoke to our hearts and moved us to share our feelings for the earth with you.

Teaching Kids to Love the Earth

C O N T E N T S

Curiosity is the starting point of learning. Curiosity is an eagerness for knowledge. For children, curiosity provides the incentive to investigate the world. And investigate they must. They need to discover who can be trusted, what is dangerous and what is fun. Children need to establish boundaries. This early learning is intense and full of action. Curiosity will, for example, lead them to the shore of a lake. They will touch the water, splash it, drink it, squeeze it, pour it. They will learn about the water through this activity. They will acquire vast amounts of information in short periods of time.

An adult's enthusiasm for learning can be as intense as a child's. Maturity is not the end of awe and wonder. Intense, curiosity-inspired learning can be sustained throughout life. Northern Minnesota explorer and naturalist Sigurd Olson wrote:

> While we are born with curiosity and wonder . . . such inherent joys are often lost. I also know that, being deep within us, their latent glow can be fanned to flame again by awareness and an open mind.

To fan the flame of curiosity, be spontaneous. Follow instincts and interests. The activities in this section of the book are designed to capitalize on our curiosity and let it lead to fun and learning.

Curiosity is the invitation to explore. If you follow the curiosity of the child within you, the glow of wonder will be fanned to flame.

CURIOSITY

1. Serentripity

Children are remarkably competent human beings. Sure, they spill juice, track mud across the kitchen, fuss over mosquito bites and pick fights with their brothers and sisters—but so do adults.

If given the chance, little people can also paddle canoes, discover intricate spider webs, wash camp dishes and create sensitive poems and pictures. Children can be strong partners—even leaders—in the outdoors.

If you respect the leadership of children you will accomplish amazing feats—feats like boulder jumping and agate finding and ant studying.

The success of this activity depends on your ability to become one in spirit with the children. During a Serentripity outing it is more important to be in tune with the children's feelings than to adhere to a prescribed lesson plan.

Serentripity: The Story

July 14. It was a cold summer day at Lake Superior. Frigid waves, driven by a powerful northeast wind, spilled over the shore.

But to those who were dressed to play along its shore, the lake's energy was contagious.

"I want to be leader first, Dad," said eight-year-old Galen.

"OK, go for it," said Paul.

Galen led Ben, Brian and Ramona out of the "fort"—a huge crevice formed in the granite by an eternity of thawing and freezing along the lakeshore.

Paul helped the three-year-olds up an alternate route. Once on the "roof" of their gigantic fort, Galen lay belly down to peer into a rainwater pool. "Come on, Dad, hurry up," he commanded. Paul hustled the three-year-olds over another crevice.

Sally promptly sat on a rock with a determined look on her face. And young Carolyn just held on tighter than ever to Paul's hand.

Galen and the older kids sped off to search for agates down on the pebble beach. Galen yelled, "Dad, look at this neat agate I found!"

Meanwhile, Eva had joined Sally in permanent residence on the rock. The game's fate was clearly sealed.

"Galen, you go ahead and keep being leader! I've got to stay here with the girls." Paul shouted above the roar of the waves. "They just can't

keep up with you."

Paul turned around to find the little girls peering between two boulders.

"Look what Sally found!" yelled Eva. Paul lay down and joined them in admiring a spider's web that imprisoned a dozen bugs. The foursome speculated on where the spider was, how the bugs had gotten stuck, why the web was hidden down in the boulders.

Sally gained courage and scampered off toward the lake, but in the opposite direction from the older kids who were still searching for beautiful agates. She skillfully pulled her slender 37 inches to the top of a boulder twice that high and stood silhouetted against the thundering gray-green waves. "LAKE SUPERIOR!" she screamed at the top of her lungs.

Carolyn and Eva wandered over and demanded access to Sally's perch. Then all three of them joined in raucous chorus, "LAAAAKKE SUUPPEERIOOORRR!"

A gull flew past and landed nearby. One by one the girls slid down and moved toward the wary bird. It wisely took flight when the trio got within 10 yards. As quickly as the wind carried the gull out over the waves, the girls' attention shifted to the "fort" they had earlier discovered with the older kids.

Paul pretended not to be watching. He climbed atop the "yelling boulder" to check on the safety of the older kids. By the time he was down again, the girls were out of sight.

"I am a hungry whale looking for something

to eat!" he roared. Giggles came from the crevice below him. Carefully hopping to a lower rock, he repeated his call. This time the gigglers gave themselves away.

"How did you get in there?" asked the whale. More giggles came from the girls as the whale scrunched himself up to fit into the crevice.

"Dad, we want to play hide-and-seek," came a voice from above.

Ramona, Ben, Brian and Galen clambered down to peek into the hiding place. The little girls proudly showed it off and let each of the older kids take a turn inside.

"Who wants to play hide-and-seek?" asked Paul.

A resounding "Me!" followed.

"The little girls and I will be it. We'll count to 25—one, two, three, four. . . ." Four pairs of legs danced up the rocks and disappeared onto the outcropping above. Eva, Carolyn and Sally lay their heads on Paul's lap and counted with him. Protected from the fury of wind and waves above them, the foursome gathered energy for the new adventure.

Activity

Purpose	To playfully foster a child's curiosity.
Age/Number/Setting	Some activities are best if spontaneous. Anyone of any age can play Serentripity.
Materials	None
How-To	Let a special child in your life be your leader. When a child shows curiosity about some natural object, drop everything and join in the investigation.
	For example, if the child begins to follow an ant, join the excursion, offering encouraging questions like: "Where do you think he is going?" "Does he live in a house like ours?"
	Similarly, follow an adult who shows curiosity. The challenge is greater here. Whereas a child will almost automatically follow his

curiosity, an adult will most likely have to be coaxed into following through on an initial expression of curiosity. Suppose a friend expresses awe and wonder at the color and form of a newly emerging mushroom. Rather than being content to mutter the usual, "That is really neat!" affirmation, get down on all fours. Look underneath the cap and talk about it: "Look, it's a different color underneath. I wonder how many there are around here?"

When do you stop encouraging the curiosity of your child, spouse or friend and move on to something new? Only you can decide.

> The whirling masses of red and yellow filled me with excitement . . . color and beauty became part of my life.
>
> **Sigurd Olson**

Did You Know?
Parents Were Important to Famous Naturalists

Many well-known naturalists attribute the longevity of their curiosity to the presence of a playful, encouraging adult in their childhood. Minnesota naturalist Sigurd Olson recalled his first sense of wonder experience in his book, *Singing Wilderness:*

> My first recollection came one sunny afternoon when Mother led me through a grove of maples in the fall. That day the trees must have been in full color, for the ground was deep in drifting leaves. As we walked through them we were surrounded with color, and when the wind blew we were drenched with it. The whirling masses of red and yellow filled me with excitement, and when we ran through the grove we ran and ran until we could run no more and sank laughing to the ground—color and beauty became part of my life.

Olson's life was an immersion in the sense of wonder about the wilds of northern Wisconsin, Minnesota and Canada. But his experiences, his introduction to the beauty and marvels of the world around him, began on an autumn hike with his mother.

In her adult life, Rachel Carson wrote *Under the Sea-Wind*, *The Edge of the Sea* and *The Sea Around Us*. But her interest in the natural world began in the lower Allegheny Valley on a 65-acre farm. The woods and fields surrounding the farm were an unending source of mystery. In *The House of Life*, Paul Brooks quoted Rachel Carson:

> I can remember no time when I wasn't interested in the outdoors and the whole world of nature. Those interests, I know, I inherited from my mother and have always shared with her. I was rather a solitary child and spent a great deal of time in woods and beside streams, learning the birds and the insects and flowers.

Across the Atlantic Ocean lie the boyhood haunts of another famous naturalist, John Muir. He grew up in Dunbar, Scotland, a seaport facing the rugged North Sea. Grandfather Gilrye walked through town with two-year-old John to Lord Lauderdale's formal gardens. Then they rested in neighboring haycocks. As John grew older, Grandfather followed him as he raced up the brae to his favorite playground—the moss-covered ruins of old Dunbar castle. In *The Story of My Boyhood and Youth*, John Muir recalled:

> I loved to wander in the fields to hear the birds sing and along the seashore to gaze and wonder at the shells and seaweeds, eels and crabs in the pools along the rocks when the tide was low, and best of all to watch the waves in awful storms thundering on the black headlands and craggy ruins of old Dunbar castle where the sea and sky, the waves and the clouds were mingled together as one.

Curiosity is an emotion, a mood. Spontaneity is the key to your outing.

As an adult, indulge yourself in the curiosity of children. Take a free-flight romp with them through a city park. Wade in a small stream. Play in a mud puddle.

Remember, curiosity is an emotion, a mood. Spontaneity is the key to your outing.

Other Ideas
For Following Your Curiosity

1. A neighborhood creek provides the perfect opportunity for letting curiosity flow. Launch a toy sailboat and allow a couple of hours to follow it downstream.

2. Follow a leader on bikes. Is there a bike trail nearby, a long hill, a particularly scenic route?

3. Take a Serentripity car outing with your family or a small group of friends. In the spirit of the trip everyone gets a chance to choose a direction to travel and a stopping place of interest.

4. In the winter or after a spring rain, follow deer or other animal tracks. Where do they stop? What changes in length of stride do you find? Do they lead to a home? Were they pursued?

5. In your small group give each person 10 pieces of surveyor's tape. Let each person lay out a similar length trail through the woods. Pair up and follow another person's trail while she follows yours. Variation: Time the trail runs.

6. Follow a night sound until you locate the source (an owl, frogs, crickets).

7. Create a hiking club. Each person takes a turn selecting an area where everyone will hike. Go as a group of adults or families.

8. Blindfold someone and take him to a place he is familiar with. Guide him around until he correctly identifies the place.

9. Make soap bubbles (1/8 cup of dish soap plus 1 cup of water). Using a blow ring, become a bubble machine. Have fun following the bubbles wherever they drift.

10. Play follow the leader on a canoe trip. The leader should be in the back of the canoe. Make sure each person takes a turn in the stern.

Resources

The Sense of Wonder by Rachel Carson. New York: Harper & Row Publishers, 1956.

The House of Life: Rachel Carson At Work by Paul Brooks. Boston: Houghton-Mifflin, 1972.

The Singing Wilderness by Sigurd F. Olson. New York: Alfred A. Knopf, 1956.

The Story of My Boyhood and Youth by John Muir. Madison: University of Wisconsin Press, 1965.

Speaking for Nature: How Literary Naturalists from Henry Thoreau to Rachel Carson Have Shaped America by Paul Brooks. Boston: Houghton-Mifflin, 1980.

The Curious Naturalist by John Mitchell. Englewood Cliffs, NJ: Prentice-Hall, Inc., 1980.

Paddle-to-the-Sea by Holling Clancy Holling. Boston: Houghton-Mifflin, 1941.

A Time of Wonder by Robert McClosky. New York: Viking Press, 1987.

Your Big Backyard and *Ranger Rick* magazines. National Wildlife Federation. 1412 16th Street NW, Washington DC 20036.

2. Abberwocky

Did you ever take the time to watch children play in their world of make-believe? The play often begins with "Let's pretend that. . . ." Energy builds as dress-up clothes are donned, toys are arranged, and roles are assigned. Real-world concerns like hunger, music lessons and chores vanish.

You, too, can open the door into the world of make-believe. Take off your watch. Find some favorite children and go outdoors. Follow your curiosity, your imagination.

In the following story, Ann kindles children's curiosity and imagination about the outdoors by conjuring up an imaginary creature. She invites four children to help her track the creature along a neighborhood creek.

Abberwocky: The Story

"Today I'd like to tell you a story about a very special creature who has been seen recently along Chester Creek," Ann said. "And then we're going looking for him!"

Her four students ranged in age from three-and-a-half to eight. With a brief reminder to pay attention to the story so they would know what clues to look for, she began.

"A long time ago, before your moms and dads were born, a most unusual baby creature was born in Lake Superior. His name was Abberwocky. He grew very fast. When he was as old as Brian ('How old is that?' . . . 'Three!'), he was already the size of your house. His eyes were as big as 10 beachballs all glued together. His skin was green and slimy. Abberwocky looked like a dinosaur, but there was something about him that made him different from every other creature in Lake Superior. Do you know what it was? (Brief discussion, with theories ranging from 'he couldn't swim' to 'he had no teeth.')

"The thing that made him different is that he liked people. All of his aunts, uncles, cousins and grandparents hated people. They would try to scare people by making loud noises. (How would a sea monster sound?) Sometimes they would make big waves and try to sink boats.

"But not Abberwocky. He just loved children. Instead of spending his time chasing human beings as his cousins did, Abberwocky spent his time exploring the streams and rivers

that flow into Lake Superior. In fact, just yesterday someone reported a huge creature walking along Chester Creek right over here.

"So, I thought that today we could go exploring up the creek looking for signs of Abberwocky," Ann concluded.

The kids were on their feet and ready to race to the stream.

Once there, Ann laid down some very strict rules: "Everyone must get their feet wet. Please share with the rest of us any monster signs you see. Be careful on slippery rocks."

The first one to wade into the stream was four-year-old Keegan. The others, seeing that the water was no deeper than Keegan's knees, immediately followed. The excitement of being in the water led them upstream.

"Hey, what is this green stuff?" Ann asked.

"Monster hair," replied eight-year-old Ramona. There was lots of it growing on the rocks, plenty for each kid to hold.

"Why is it growing all over the rocks?" Ann asked.

"The rocks scraped it off Abberwocky," answered Keegan.

Under some of the rocks they found sacks of eggs covered with a jelly-like stuff. The kids decided Abberwocky had laid eggs in the stream.

In another place on the edge of the stream they found a bunch of foot-long, brown, rotten objects piled up.

"Mommy, what is this?" asked Brian, the

youngest detective.

"What do you guys think?"

The kids waded out of the water and crowded around.

"Poop," said Galen matter-of-factly. "It's Abberwocky's poop."

The kids roared. Ann could see that Galen felt bad.

"I think Galen is right," she said. "Monsters have to poop just like any animal. Now that we're out of the water, what other signs can we see that show us a monster the size of a house was walking along this stream?"

The kids looked around at the birch and maple forest and were obviously puzzled. Ann asked them if Abberwocky had a tail. The conclusion was resounding: "Yes!" When Ann pointed out all of the trees that were shedding bark, they quickly decided that the monster's tail had been bumping it off the trees.

"Wow! Abberwocky knocked down this tree!" said Ramona.

"Could he do that?" Ann asked. "Let's go and see if we could knock it the rest of the way over." They couldn't, of course, but they were sure that Abberwocky could.

For 90 minutes they scoured Chester Creek, examining everything for a sign of Abberwocky.

For example, a place next to the stream where all the grass had been matted down was his footprint. But then they came to the Kenwood Avenue bridge.

"Where do you suppose Abberwocky went from here?" Ann asked.

It was obvious to the kids that he was too big to go through the culvert. On the other hand, they were sure he was too scared of people to climb up the bank and walk across the road. Ann suggested they hike out to the trail and climb the hill to see if a better view would give them some ideas.

Sitting atop the hill that overlooks the stream, Ann asked, "Do you think Abberwocky can fly?" No doubt in their minds. "Where could he fly to?"

"Up in the clouds," said Keegan.

"Yeah, right up there is a cloud big enough to hold him," said Ramona.

Ramona, Keegan, Galen, Brian and Ann sat and watched clouds for some time, finding a great assortment of monsters hiding in the fast-moving summer clouds.

"Can we come back tomorrow and look for Abberwocky?" asked Brian.

"Yeah, I'm gonna bring my mom!" said Keegan.

Activity

Purpose To let imagination lead participants on a wet-footed hike.

Age/Number/Setting This is best suited for the eight-and-under crowd, those still able to believe in monsters. A group totaling fewer than six children and adults works best.

Materials You will need transportation to a stream, wading shoes for everyone and a ready-made introductory story about the monster that lives in your stream.

How-To Tell a monster story with enthusiasm. Have the monster possess unique qualities for your special stream—for example, he may love rock cliffs or water lilies or other features particular to your stream. Keep the initial story short. Begin your hike and keep telling the story as you go.

Assume a playful spirit. You are free from the responsibility of putting realistic names on anything: insect eggs on the undersides of rocks can be monster eggs; a tree trunk shed of bark by a woodpecker can be a monster's rubbing post; a deer's bed can be a monster's footprint.

Offer the children plenty of questions but no preconceived answers.

Needless to say, you're a detective, too. A dry-footed leader sitting on a rock you cannot be.

Did You Know?
Imagination Sparks Magic

As parents, we are drawn to the imaginative play and freedom of our children. With them we can talk to trees, follow creeks in search of Abberwocky, touch flowers while looking for dancing ladies, and hear the eerie calls of sea monsters in ocean breezes.

Letting go of the facts, we let the energy and spirit of our children carry us along into the wonderful world of make-believe.

Imagination is movement. It can help us explore the mysterious and miraculous natural world. Flying on the wings of imagination, we can travel to old places in new ways. A bracken-fern forest can become a place for stalking fairies on our knees.

Or imagination can enable us to be brave explorers of new horizons. Look beyond a broad-winged hawk circling above a field. Close your eyes and take flight. Circle with the hawk as it searches for food. Extend your arms, sway in the prevailing winds and climb the thermals. Whether used in a simple game of charades or during a quiet moment under an oak tree with a group of friends, imagination can move you to experience the natural world in ways that mere observation cannot.

Imagination is enhanced by myth. In designing our Sense of Wonder workshops, we use myths and legends to aid in our investigation of the natural world. In red plaid shirts and wool pants we have joined Paul Bunyan and Babe to hunt the infamous Hodag monster in the waters and piney woods of northern Wisconsin. Whole families have been recruited as lumberjacks to experience the logging era of the Northwoods. Donning sashes, knit hats and French accents, we have been voyageurs exploring the waterways of Northern Minnesota. Paddling canoes and

A
bracken-fern forest
can become a
place
for stalking
fairies
on our knees.

singing in the mist of a fall morning, we've gained fur traders' perspectives on beaver dams and lodges.

Whether you recreate an existing legend, or craft a new one of your own, share the message by retelling it for and with neighbors and friends.

Other Ideas
For Using Your Imagination

1. Along the beach there are plenty of natural history signs that can bring a sea monster to life. Take pails and shovels to collect the evidence.

2. Build a sand castle while relating a story about its fictitious inhabitants. Build a city of critters to go with the castle.

3. While walking along a northern beach in the fall, search for the migration of ladybugs. Ponder how they got there, where they're going, how they'll survive winter.

4. After taking a hike, paddle or bike ride, find a place to play animal charades. Have everyone choose to mime an animal or plant they saw signs of that day.

5. Create a story to explain an interesting natural phenomenon such as why birds fly south.

6. Have a Paul Bunyan contest. Find the largest tree in a given area. Your "tape measure" is how many people can fit around the tree.

7. Pass a candle around a group. Have each candle bearer add to a make-believe story about what might happen on the next day's outing.

8. Spread a plastic tarp on a sloped lawn. Run a hose at the top and turn on the water. Use plastic sleds and kids in swimsuits to create an otter slide.

9. Lie down under a tree. Look up and imagine what it feels like to be a tree—home to birds and squirrels. Think about fluttering in the wind like a leaf and falling to the ground. Imagine that you are a drop of water traveling up the tree from its roots.

Resources

Choosing Books for Kids: Choosing the Right Book for the Right Child at the Right Time by Joanne Oppenheim, Barbara Brenner and Betty Boegehold. New York: Ballantine Books, 1986.

The New Read-Aloud Handbook by Jim Trelease. New York: Penguin Books, 1989.

The Use of Enchantment: The Meaning and Importance of Fairy Tales by Bruno Bettelheim. New York: Alfred A. Knopf, 1976.

Keepers of the Earth by Michael J. Caduto and Joseph Bruchae. Golden, CO: Fulcrum Inc., 1988.

Where the Wild Things Are by Maurice Sendak. Harper & Row, 1963.

The Fairy Tale Treasury collected by Virginia Haviland. New York: Dell, 1986.

Paul Bunyan adapted by Steven Kellogg. New York: Morrow, 1984.

The Hobbit by J.R.R. Tolkien. New York: Ballantine,1988.

Pond and Brook: A Guide to Nature Study in Freshwater Environments by Michael Caduto. Englewood Cliffs, NJ: Prentice-Hall, 1985.

The Life of Rivers and Streams by Rovert Usinger, New York: McGraw-Hill, 1967.

CURIOSITY

Curiosity
is the
starting point
of
learning.

3. By the Light of the Moon

Darkness is a time not commonly explored. It is unknown and mysterious, a time of awe and fear.

In this story we see a group of people deal openly and support-ively with their fear of darkness. In a guided activity that involves howling for wolves, teenager Christopher's fear actually helps create a night of heightened awareness.

You can also adapt this activity into an owl call or a watch for shooting stars.

By the Light of the Moon: The Story

"You don't have to howl," 14-year-old Christopher's mom said to him in their dormitory room. "Besides, I think all the rest of us will be adults. You won't be embarassing yourself out in front of any of your buddies."

Three hours later, 10 p.m., Environmental Learning Center, Isabella, Minnesota; a partly cloudy February night. A group of 15 set out on foot around Flathorn Lake to go wolf howling.

"It's okay to talk until we get to the far side of the lake, but after that there can be absolutely no talking," said Ann.

"This is tricky walking," said Christopher to his new friend Becky.

The group wasn't exclusively adults after all. But Christopher didn't mind.

"No kidding. I don't know why we can't turn on some flashlights," Becky answered. Both were uncomfortable with the clumsy gait the snow-packed trail imposed on them. Neither dared mention how ill at ease they felt among the dark shadows of the forest. Their talk drifted to comparing high schools.

The group spread itself out over the undulating trail but closed ranks when the leader stopped at a footbridge. When Christopher and Becky, the only teenagers in the group, arrived, Christopher's parents were at the front, visiting with the leader. The other adults were mingling in groups of two and three.

"Can everyone see this?" asked Ann. The group gathered around to see what she was pointing at in the snow. "These are fresh wolf tracks. Can anyone figure out why they might be so large?"

An adult voice under a stocking cap answered, "So that the wolves can run quickly over the snow in pursuit of deer."

"Great!" responded Ann. "At this point we are standing on the boundary of two wolf packs. The one off to the northwest did not raise a successful litter last year. They are just five in number. The one behind us is now up to 12."

"What are we supposed to do if the wolves come?" whispered Becky to Christopher.

"Ask Ann."

"I'd feel too dumb."

"What happens if the wolves come to check us out?" Christopher finally asked.

"Good question. For some reason, that question is almost never asked by adults. But I know they're thinking about it!" said Ann. "If the wolves come, we're lucky. We would get to see what I believe to be the most perfect symbol of wildness that can be found in the lower 48 states."

In the long silence that followed there was an occasional foot shuffle or throat clearing. But mostly 15 people were listening to the quickened beat of their own hearts. Ann relieved the tension. "With this many howlers I doubt that the wolves will get close, but they could," she said. "Last summer a group of howlers had a whole pack come to the edge of the woods. The pack stared at them for a long time and then returned to the forest."

11 p.m. The nearly full moon made more appearances through the light cloud cover. The leafless birch trees painted eerie silhouettes against the sky. The scattered spruces towered in menacing silence.

"What did they do when the wolves got that close?" asked Christopher's mom.

"Froze," Ann said in a whisper. "The person who told the story said that only when the wolves finally turned to go did it occur to him that he had been spared because he was human. Wolves will kill other wolves who venture into their territory."

Christopher's cool teenage poise was shattered by the story. He was grateful for the cover of darkness. He stepped forward to close the group's circle.

"No more questions for awhile," said Ann. "We'll walk about a half-mile in complete silence. Then I'll howl three times, waiting about five minutes between howls. If we get no response, then we'll move to another spot."

Thirty feet crunched the snow on the path. Thirty feet in close ranks. No one talked. Christopher wondered how 15 relative strangers could honor so much silence, could feel such unity of purpose. His mind wandered . . . until he heard the first howl.

The hair stood up on the back of his neck. He felt the forest closing in. Silence. Then another, "hoooooooooowl." He could almost hear the footsteps of the four-legged creatures behind the row of spruces to his left.

Another howl from Ann.

Though Christopher had never heard a wolf howl, he was sure it was a perfect imitation. His parents had often taken him on night walks in the past, but their focus had been the beauty of silence and the development of senses other than sight. Never had they tried to bring forth the spirit of fear. And now Christopher was genuinely scared.

"It should be a perfect night for a response," whispered Ann. "There is little wind to block out the wolves' answer. Let's move down the trail a short distance and howl again. This time I want you to join me."

Christopher could not bring himself to howl, but he heard Becky try. And he heard his mom's high-pitched call. He felt only relief that the night answered with silence.

By the third round of calls, Christopher relaxed some. He even muttered a half-hearted howl on the last chorus.

"Did you hear that?" asked an older man standing next to Christopher.

"Yes, I think I did," answered Ann. "Let's try a couple more howls."

Christopher strained his ears after the echoes of their human howls fell silent. "Nah, couldn't be. We're just hearing things because we want to," he thought. But he knew he had heard something.

The sound answered them only twice more.

"I think we had a wolf answer us," said Ann. "It was pretty faint and far off, though. What you heard is the sound of some of the last wild wolves in America. As we head back, think about these creatures. Why are there so few?

Why is this one of the last places wolves can be found? Let us maintain silence until we are back to the dorms. I would like you to reflect on the special magic of this night. If there are questions you want to ask, I'll be glad to answer them when we get back."

Christopher's curiosity was aroused. What had the answering howls meant? Were they from one wolf or several? Could anybody go out and howl for wolves? What were the real dangers? He could hardly contain his questions.

Two hours ago he had been the skeptical teenager. Now he was the eager student, ready to explore, to try it again.

Activity

Purpose To go on a night expedition. By all means, a howling expedition if you're in wolf country.

Age/Number/Setting Age six through adult. Maximum of 15. A moonlit (but not necessarily full-moon) night.

Materials Appropriate night-time clothing and good shoes or boots.

How-To Respect and deal openly with fear of the night. Discuss common feelings before and during a night outing. Temper fears with knowledge. For example, if an outing to go wolf howling is preceded with an information session on why wolves howl and what their howling means, fears will be minimized. The dangers will be understood and real instead of imaginary.

For this activity, obtain information on the location of wolf packs in the area you would like to explore. Contact the nearest U.S. Forest Service or state department of natural resource's wildlife biologist for up-to-date information. These professionals may refer you to someone else, but they will usually be aware of who in your area is most knowledgeable.

There are few experienced "howlers." Fortunately, to get a response, your howl needn't be particularly professional. Practice howling out loud so you won't feel silly when you let go with your best in the silence of the north woods. A long, loud "hoooooooooowl" will do.

The recommended procedure is simple. Howl, wait a couple of minutes, howl, wait a couple of minutes, howl again and then wait a couple more minutes.

Follow the example of the leader in the story. Set the mood with your group. Keep everyone silent and serious. Capitalize on the magic of being outdoors at night.

Did You Know?
The Wolf Symbolizes Wildness

Temper fears with knowledge.

Weighing from 80 to 172 pounds, the wolf is *the* primary non-human predator of this nation's moose, elk and deer. Although these powerful creatures have a fundamental fear of people, folk tales from the earliest recorded myths and legends often cast wolves as evil, vicious and dangerous. It is safe to say that no other endangered species is the victim of as much incorrect information.

Minnesota has the largest free-roaming population of wolves in the lower 48 states. In addition to the 1,200 wolves in the northern third of the state, there are about 20 on Isle Royale National Park in Lake Superior and about three dozen in the Upper Peninsula of Michigan and northern Wisconsin. There are about 50,000 wolves in Canada and another 10,000 or so in Alaska.

The
moon
has
nothing to do
with
wolves'
conversations.

In 1915 wolves lived in all states. But that year Congress passed a law that encouraged the extermination of wolves on federal lands. Wolves were then systematically and efficiently killed. Traps, guns, poison and dogs were used in the war against wolves. By 1967 the wolf was considered eliminated from all of the lower 48 states except Minnesota. In 1973 the wolf was added to the federal list of endangered species. However, in 1978 its protected status was weakened from "endangered" to "threatened." A move is now afoot to create a sport hunting season for a limited number of the animals in the state of Minnesota.

Wolves do not howl because there is a full moon. They howl to announce themselves, to assert territorial claims and to call meetings. The moon has nothing to do with wolves' conversations. However, if you are attempting to speak to them, it is nice for *you* to have the advantage of a little light. Wolves will respond to human calls. In fact, in 1985 one Minnesota Department of Natural Resources researcher was so effective at calling them that he was able to map successfully all wolf territories in a 300-square-mile area, using only the information he gained from howling.

Sometime in the early 1990s the Science Museum of Minnesota's wolf exhibit will find a permanent home. Complete with a living wolf pack and extensive historical background, this exhibit will be well worth seeing. Standing as a magnificent symbol of wildness, the wolf can do much to spark a sense of wonder. This symbol of fear can also serve as a symbol of concern for the wilderness.

Other Ideas
For Overcoming Fears

1. Join an organized owl prowl through your local nature center or Audubon group. Use tape-recorded owl sounds or hoot to solicit a response.

2. Find out exactly what time the full moon will rise. Take your family or a small group of friends to a scenic overlook or beach to watch it.

3. Choose a place where you feel comfortable during the daytime and visit it at night. A moon walk will heighten the use of other senses and provide an unforgettable experience. Bring a family member or friend along with you for support.

4. Stargazing can weave a certain magic to allay fears of the night. Lie down in your backyard or at a park or campsite. Find a group of stars and make a picture out of it. Describe your picture to friends or family members. Help them find it. (A powerful flashlight for pointing is helpful.) Make up a story about how the object got in the sky.

5. Give someone in your group a whistle and tell him to hide and blow the whistle every minute or two. See if your family or group of friends can find the person who is hiding as you follow your ears to the spot.

6. Snorkeling in the shallows of a lake provides a chance to see the beauty of the underwater world and to minimize the fear of what it contains.

7. A snow cave built in the comfort of your own backyard provides an easy introduction to the world of winter camping. Its cozy interior is a gentle reminder that fear of survival in the winter can be overcome.

Resources

Of Wolves and Men by Barry Lopez. New York: Charles Scribner's Sons, 1978.

White Wolf: Living with an Arctic Legend by Jim Brandenberg. Minocqua, WI: Northword Press, Inc., 1988.

The Wolf: The Ecology and Behavior of an Endangered Species by David Mech. New York: The Natural History Press, 1970.

Never Cry Wolf by Farley Mowat. New York: Bantam, 1963.

Nightlife: Nature from Dusk to Dawn by Diana Kappel-Smith. Boston: Little, Brown and Company, 1990.

The Nocturnal Naturalist: Exploring the Outdoors at Night by Cathy Johnson. Chester, CT: Globe Peqout Press, 1989.

Little People of the Night by Laura Bannon. Boston: Houghton-Mifflin Company, 1963.

Julie of the Wolves , by Jean Craighead George. New York: Harper, 1972.

Walk When the Moon is Full by Frances Hamerstrom. New York: The Crossing Press, 1975.

Owl Moon by Jane Yolen. New York: Putnam, 1987. Harper & Row, 1972.

Large as Life: Nighttime Animals by Joanne Cole. Alfred A. Knopf, 1985.

Everyone is an explorer. While some people explore distant lands and galaxies, others explore their own backyards. While some enjoy exploring wild places, others prefer exploring relationships with people. Some people are fond of careful investigations and directed travel; others are masters of chance and thrive on serendipity. The astronomer explores stars; the philosopher explores ideas. We are all explorers—fascinated by the new, intrigued by the mysterious and captivated by the challenge of learning and doing.

Exploration is an investigation of the world. It is looking at new things and new places. It is also seeing the old in new ways. Exploration is doing. It is active, playful and dynamic. It is exhilarating when you come so close to what you're investigating that you become a part of it. You get lost in the moment.

Imagine a backpacker walking down a dry stream bed. She stops momentarily. What is underfoot? Kneeling down, her hand touches the sand. She digs down. Gravel. Deeper yet, she discovers pebbles. Deeper still, her fingers are stopped by large stones.

As she explores, more questions come. What forces built the stream bed? Why is each layer so different and distinct? What role did the water play? Where did the water go? Why isn't it here any more?

Curiosity arouses your interest in something—such as a stream bed. Exploration is the activity of taking the time to pursue the answers to the questions that your curiosity raises.

The activities in this section provide a variety of ways for you to explore your world and the mysteries that surround you. Exploration invites you on a journey that can lead you in many directions. The only obstacle to exploration is your door.

Open it. And explore!

EXPLORATION

EXPLORATION

Exploration
is a journey
that can
lead
in many
directions.

4. Predator/Prey

The key to exploration is time outdoors. One of the most effective
ways to get people, particularly children, outdoors is to offer them
the chance to play. Games that teach ecological concepts provide
an enjoyable way to help children explore.

Everyone has played hide-and-go-seek. In this exciting outdoor
version of that ever-popular game, participants of all ages gain an
animal's perspective in the exploration of a new habitat.

Predator/Prey: The Story

"I see you, Ann!" yelled Amber. Ann stood up in the dried grass and walked over to the red-tailed hawk "predator." Amber was the red-tailed hawk. "I saw your head moving," she told Ann.

But strain though she might, six-year-old Amber could not see Brian or Galen. She was discouraged, so Ann reminded her that she could ask them to stand up and move in closer while she had her eyes closed. Brian was hiding behind a small spruce, and Galen was behind a boulder. They were mice. Ann and Amber closed their eyes and counted out loud to 20.

Brian and Galen had vanished. "It isn't fair. They're too good," announced Amber.

"How do you think hawks find prey when they're hungry?" asked Ann. "It's hard work finding mice and gophers to eat."

"Yeah, but they're flying up high and can see better than me."

"You're right about that. How about if we try thinking where would be the best place for those two mice to hide? Remember, they have to be hiding in closer than last time."

Six-year-old Brian had played this game many times. At first he wouldn't hide alone. Even now he got upset if he was found too early. That wouldn't happen today; he had changed into his camouflage pants before coming.

Seven-year-old Galen was a pro at this game. He was the born naturalist of the group. He was the kind of kid who was just as happy sitting for 15 minutes waiting for a chickadee to take seed out of his hand as he was building a snow fort or sledding.

In the first round of the game, when Brian was the hawk, Galen got caught right away because of his maroon jacket. But he learned about camouflage. This time he was lying flat against the fall earth without his jacket on.

"Wow! Look at that!" Galen stood straight up and pointed to the sky.

"I got you, Galen," announced Amber, a newcomer to this game.

But Galen paid no attention. "Ann, look! I think those are peregrine falcons." Ann ran over to the spot where Galen stood and followed his finger to two diving falcons high above the ridge next to them.

"Oh, my gosh, I think you're right! Let me get the binoculars."

The binoculars proved Galen to be correct. The birds had long pointed wings, slender tails and dark caps.

"Mom, I never got to see them so good before," said Brian. "Can I be it now and be a peregrine falcon?"

"Sure," said Ann. "Start counting to 20."

Ann found a spot behind a boulder, lay on her back and searched for another glimpse of the diving falcons. She turned over again to see Brian. She thought she had been careful.

"I got you!"

Ann walked over to where Brian was standing. "You're a pretty sharp hawk," she announced. Brian beamed and started looking for the others.

After Amber and Galen had been caught, Ann gathered the kids in a circle.

"Why were we hiding?" reviewed Ann.

Amber said, "To learn about predators and prey."

Galen added, "We were using our camouflage to hide."

"What prey were those two peregrine falcons after?" asked Ann.

"Mice," said Brian.

"Little birds," said Galen.

"Good guesses," said Ann. "Do you think they had any luck?" That stumped the young naturalists. Amber, not as confident as Brian and Galen, saw a chance to say something.

"No."

Galen added, "Amber's right 'cause we didn't see them stop flying or anything."

Ann complimented the kids on their playing ability and announced that it was time to head home.

Halfway back to the car the falcons staged a return performance. The kids stopped momentarily but then continued down the trail. Ann couldn't move. Her eyes followed the two birds until they became small, black specks over Lake Superior.

Activity

Purpose
: To use a game of hide-and-seek to better understand how animals act.

Age/Number/Setting
: Any age can play. Adults can have a lot of fun, as can mixed-age groups—even families with preschoolers. If you're playing with preschoolers, pair them up with someone older as their hiding partner. Group size can vary from three or four people to a couple of dozen. Because everyone must remain still for minutes at a time, the game is best played when it's not so cold or wet so that sitting quietly will become uncomfortable. But the game can be good in winter! We have played at 20 degrees in snowsuits and enjoyed it. A field or wood lot is a good place to play.

Materials   Flagging to mark the predator "perch" and the boundaries of the playing area. Clothing that blends in with the surroundings.

How-To   Select a site that is relatively free from hazards like poison ivy, cliffs or deep water, but which provides potentially good hiding places.

Ask questions. "What kind of animals do you think live here?" Generate a long list—include everything from butterflies and frogs to deer and hawks. "Who knows what a predator is?" Someone surely will, even in the under-five crowd. "What predators live here?" "Who knows what a prey is?" You will undoubtedly list some creatures that are difficult to classify. For example, how do you classify a shrew that is eaten by hawks but eats insects? This will give you an opportunity to talk about the importance of each creature's role in maintaining nature's balance.

The game has only a few rules. First, there are boundaries. It will be helpful for you to walk around the perimeter of the game area while everyone is watching. After you have done that, return to the center of the circle at the predator's "perch." You may also choose to flag the boundaries of the game circle (50- to 100-foot radius, depending upon the vegetation) before beginning the game.

As leader, you may want to be the predator first, especially with a group of children. The subtleties of rules like having everyone move in after the first round are hard to remember. Children will want to be "it" the next time around. So be prepared with a method for choosing the next predator.

Explain the rules briefly. "I will cover my eyes and count to 20. Find a place to hide where you can see me at all times." (This rule will go a long way toward preventing lost kids.) "When I get to 20, I will sound my predator's call. If I see you, I will point at you and call. Then you must stand up and come join me." (When they come join you, don't let them help find others until the next round of hiding.) "When I can't find anyone else, I'll say,

'Everyone stand up where you are.' Then those at the predator perch with me will keep their eyes closed and count to 20 while the prey creatures move in closer and hide again."

The game continues until everyone is caught or until the predator gives up.

At the end of the game gather everyone together and exchange some thoughts. "What was a good hiding place? What types of cover worked best? Was camouflage used? How did it feel to be a "predator?" With kids keep this talking session brief since they will want to play another round. Play the game as many times as feels right for the group.

With adults and teenagers it is valuable to have a good wrap-up discussion on what has been learned about predator/prey relationships that occur naturally on this piece of land. With kids the discussion is best limited to conversation on the way home.

Did You Know?
Games Help You Explore

Games are an important way of exploring the outdoors. They increase awareness of our surroundings and join us to others in a spirit of play. Cooperation, trust and caring can be reinforced through the games we play. Games can also be used to heighten sensory awareness and to teach ecological concepts, as in this game, Predator/Prey.

The game of Predator/Prey is just one of the many games we have designed to teach ecological concepts. Other games can also illustrate food webs, biological diversity and population dynamics.

Cooperation,
trust and caring
can be reinforced
through
the games
we play.

Sharing Nature with Children contains many excellent games of this type. The *Project Learning Tree, Project Wild* and *Project Wild Aquatic* activity guides are also useful. Other games can be created and used to raise players' consciousness of environmental issues and to develop the cooperative spirit needed to heal the earth.

Sensory games are plentiful. In playful and competitive ways, these contests encourage the players to identify natural objects through their use of smell, touch and hearing. *Hug a Tree* by Robert Rockwell, Elizabeth Sherwood and Robert William; *Humanizing Environmental Education* by Cliff Knapp and Joel Goodman; and *Sharing Nature with Children* by Joseph Cornell contain excellent sensory awareness activities that can be used as games.

Simulation games can be used to illustrate interactive forces at play when dealing with environmental issues. Air quality, water pollution, toxic-waste management, recycling, endangered-species management, population and land use all involve the interplay of cultural values and beliefs, technology, politics and economics.

Role playing, board games and computer programs—all based on game techniques and theory—can be used to raise players' awareness of the complexity of issues and to challenge them to identify and work toward realistic solutions. *Project Learning Tree* and *Project Wild* include interactive games like "Dragonfly Pond," which deal with resource conflicts and value dilemmas.

The number of interactive computer programs for environmental learning is growing. Perhaps the largest and most challenging game of this type is the *World Game* designed by Buckminster Fuller for the 1967 World Fair. The *World Game* is still being played through workshops offered by the World Game Institute. In the game, hundreds of participants play on a gigantic map (game board) of the world. They use information on resources and combine it with knowledge of economics, politics and ecology to develop strategies for solving world problems like hunger, housing, energy and the threat of nuclear warfare.

The *New Games Book* created an avalanche of interest in play that is noncompetitive. Its slogan was "Play Hard, Play Fair, Nobody Hurt." The New Games approach does not deal specifically with sensory awareness, ecological concepts or environmental issues. Instead it focuses on developing attributes that are prerequisites for becoming effective environmental problem-solvers and citizens of the planet Earth. New Games teach people to play together, to laugh, to cooperate and to care for each other.

In a number of New Games, participants play with a giant Earth Ball. The games of knots, people pyramids, stand-up and lap-sit bring laughter to family picnics as well as to workshops dealing with environmental problem-solving activities. Beyond that, the games are just plain fun. Two other books, *More New Games* and *Play Fair,* also contain games of this type, while *Cowstails and Cobras* emphasizes games fostering trust and cooperation.

If you can't get to a library or bookstore to check out these books, just find a kid. They know lots of games!

Games can be used to develop the cooperative spirit needed to heal the earth.

Other Ideas For Playing Environmental Games

1. Go to an area and talk about what animals live there. Determine who eats whom. Divide the group to represent each animal. Then play a game of tag—predators chasing their prey.

2. Place a dozen marbles around a small section of lawn. Tell the players how many marbles have been hidden and give participants a time limit to find them. Discuss why some marbles were easy to find and others were hard. Talk about camouflage in the plant and animal world.

3. Using map and compass, lay out an orienteering course in a field or neighborhood park. Set out stations for activities—finding objects that have different textures, smells, or sounds; writing a poem or song; planting a seed in the earth.

4. To study the migration of birds, use a compass to take your group on a pre-designed trail. Arrange three or four stopping places—a lunch stop to mimic predation, an overlook to talk about landscapes, a hidden tape recorder of bird's songs.

5. Walk to an area in the woods or in a field and use surveyors tape to mark out an imaginary habitat for a bird of prey that you choose. Construct a nest for your raptor. Hide a picture of the bird so other players can hunt for it. Prepare a story about the raptor for your group.

6. Play animal habitat hide-and-seek. Let some members of your group select an animal and create a home for it. Assign other members to look for the home. When they find it, they should try to identify what animal the home belongs to.

7. Vary your predator/prey games by varying habitat. Play in field and forest. Have everyone think about different animals that would inhabit an area and about their adaptations.

8. Play predator/prey games in different seasons. Playing the game in winter will help participants gain a real understanding of camouflage.

9. Be a pack hunter! Play predator/prey on the move. The predator moves. Prey must run to the safety of "home base." As soon as the prey is caught, he can join the leader to form a pack and hunt more prey together.

10. Play a variation of tag where you are "free" if you are touching a specific tree species.

Resources

Twilight Hunter: Wolves, Coyotes and Foxes by Gary Turbak. Flagstone, AZ: Northland Press, 1987.

A Field Guide to the Mammals by William Burt and Richard Grossenheider. Boston: Houghton Mifflin Co., 1964.

Life on Earth by David Attenborough. Boston: Little, Brown and Company, 1981.

Sharing Nature With Children by Joseph Cornell. Nevada City, CA: Dawn Publications, 1979.

Humanizing Environmental Education: A Guide for Leading Nature and Human Nature Activities by Clifford Knapp and Joel Goodman. Martinsville, IN: American Camping Association, 1981.

Hug A Tree by Robert Rockwell, Elizabeth Sherwood and Robert Williams. Mt. Ranier, WA: Gryphon House, Inc., 1983.

Project Learning Tree. The American Forest Council, 1250 Connecticut Ave., NW, Washington, DC 20036, 1979.

Project Wild. Salina Star Route, Boulder, CO 80302.

World Game. World Game Institute, University City Science Center, 3508 Market St., Philadelphia, PA 19104.

The New Games Book edited by Andrew Fluegelman. Garden City, NY: Dolphin Books, 1976.

Playfair by Matt Weinstein and Joel Goodman. San Luis Obispo: Impact Publishers, 1990.

Cowstails and Cobras by Karl Rohnke. Project Adventure, Hamilton, MA 01977.

Exploration
is a journey
that can
lead
in many
directions.

5. It's a Keeper!

The joyful companionship of an adult and a child can take the form of a walk in the woods, a canoe paddle, a fishing trip or a stroll through the garden. Where or what the adult and child explore is not as important as how they do it. Together they can keep alive their sense of wonder.

Teaching the child a skill is one of the most common ways for a parent and child to explore the outdoors together. In this story we see a lifelong fisherman teach his six-year-old daughter the patience and determination it takes to become a stream angler.

It's a Keeper: The Story

"Frank, you can't take her fishing up there!"

"Mom, I can walk that far," argued six-year-old Ann.

"She'll be fine, Astrid," assured Frank. "We'll just hike up to the beaver ponds. We won't go all the way to the falls."

"She doesn't know the first thing about fishing," tried Astrid one more time.

"But I want to learn, and Dad said when I was six, I could learn," insisted Ann.

Frank grinned and said nothing. Astrid gave up.

An hour later, at the creek, Frank said to Ann, "I'll put your hooks on, but if you're going to fish then you've got to put on your own bait. First you spear the worm like this, then you hook it several more times."

Ann watched carefully and quietly. Dad explained things only once.

"Do you see where the creek falls over ledges and logs and rocks and makes a pool?" Frank asked. Ann nodded. "That's where the trout hide. You have to be real careful not to spook 'em. We'll sneak up on that pool over there and fish it together."

Ann could barely breathe, she was so excited. She followed her dad to the stream's edge, using care not to step on any sticks. After all the years of hearing her dad tell fishing stories, *she* was actually fishing with him.

"Now you watch how I throw my line in and let it run into the pool," Dad said.

Within minutes Frank had a fighting-mad fish on his line.

"Dad! Dad! You got one! You got one!" shouted Ann.

Frank brought the trout in, carefully held the line above the fish's mouth and gave the hook a jerk.

The young trout dropped off into the water. Frank turned to his stunned daughter and explained, "He was too little, honey. We've got to let him grow bigger. Did you see that I didn't touch the fish so I wouldn't hurt him. That way he'll grow big and strong and we can catch him next year."

Ann realized that there's so much to think about—baiting hooks, finding holes, letting your line follow the water, not catching little fish. She sat and watched as quietly and patiently as she could manage. She knew that her dad didn't like questions, but after what seemed an eternity, she could wait no longer. "When do I get to fish?"

"Hand me your pole, let's see how it works here," he said.

And so they stood, side-by-side, at one hole after another. Frank would cast both of their lines and then they'd wait, in silence. Sometimes he would offer her a little advice about taking up the slack in her line or about being careful not to let her shadow be seen on the water. But mostly father and daughter shared the fellowship of their first fishing excursion without the intrusion of words.

There were no keepers that day, but many more trips followed.

By the time Ann was eight, Frank trusted her to fish holes by herself. She knew how to get her line unsnagged and rebaited. And she usually managed to catch two or three keepers each trip.

Each year Frank took her farther and farther up into the mountains, teaching her how to cross small streams safely, showing her raspberry patches he'd discovered in other years, sharing the excitement of a soaring eagle or laughter at the antics of the stream-walking water ouzel—a large bird common in the mountains.

By the time she was 12, Ann was accomplished at mountain-stream fishing. On one trip, though, Ann had a long spell with no keepers, not even any strikes. She was frustrated and more than a bit disgruntled that her dad always got to go ahead of her and try the holes first. She was determined that she was going to find a hole that wasn't yet spooked.

She caught up to Frank, half-heartedly fished a pool he had just left and watched for his move to the next hole. He bypassed a hole that was surrounded by thick brush and moved upstream.

"Now, if I can just get myself out to that pool by the brush, I know I'll catch a big one," Ann thought. She put her tennis shoes carefully one in front of the other in the cold mountain stream. Her first cast fell short of the hole. The second cast only hit the edge. The third drifted exactly to where she was sure the big one lay. Seconds ticked by. The hard push of the water

and its numbing coldness threatened to distract her. Then it happened. The gentle tugging. The curious sampling by a fish. Bam! Down went her pole.

"Oh my gosh, it's a big one!" yelled Ann. "Where am I going to land it?"

Slowly she backed up—one hand on the pole, one on rocks in the water to steady her against the force of the stream. "Please, please, don't get away," she pleaded. Two steps back she found a place where she could flip the fish up into the brush and somehow trap it if it fell off the hook. "One, two, three, go!" she yelled as she flipped the fish up behind her.

The fish disappeared into a tangle of willows —off the hook, but land-locked. Ann managed to hang onto her pole, but fell seat first into the stream when she turned to scramble on shore. She quickly got up, unaware of being soaked.

"Oh, where did he go? I've got to get him!" The willows seemed impenetrable. Ann set her pole down on the shore and began crawling through the maze of leaves and branches.

She could hear the fish but couldn't see it. Finally she trapped the fish in her hands—a beautiful 18-inch rainbow trout. "Wow! Dad will be so proud of me!"

She reached in her pocket and pulled out a stringer. "I can't believe it! It's the biggest fish I ever caught," the young, scratched-up angler yelled.

Frank was in a panic. Ann had been gone for quite a while. She hadn't answered his whistle. She didn't know it, but he always kept very close tabs on her, never letting her out of his sight for more than 20 minutes at a stretch. He had retraced his steps around the boulders and the willow thicket back to his last fishing hole. Finally he saw her tracks in the sand.

Minutes later they found each other—the beaming, wet girl proudly displayed the big fish to her worried father. He put his arm around her, grateful for her presence, her spirit and her safety. That gesture was the greatest reward Ann could have asked for.

Activity

Purpose
To share an outdoor skill with a child.

Age/Number/Setting
The child can be any age. The prerequisite is simply that he or she has shown some interest in the activity.

Materials
Young canoeists need paddles that they can manage. Berry pickers need buckets. An angler needs a pole. Providing the youngster with equipment communicates that you are taking him seriously.

How-To
Share stories of your adventures. Whether around the family dinner table or in a special one-on-one conversation, let the child know where you went, what you did, why you liked it. These conversations are the seeds of future companionship.

Wait until the child is ready. "Ready" means both interested and capable. The child is interested when he or she begins to ask permission to go along. A child is capable of learning a skill any time you have enough patience to teach it.

Break the skill down into achievable steps. If, for example, the skill is fishing and the child is barely capable of holding a pole, rig up a stick with a string and bobber and go to a small pond. Around age four or five, the child will want a "real" pole. Rig up one of your old poles with a worm and bobber or purchase an inexpensive child-sized one. At first do the casting for the child.

Regardless of the skill that is being taught, outings should be short, fun and focused entirely on the child's needs. As the child's concentration and physical coordination increase, attempt more ambitious outings.

Keep your own skills and interests alive by making time for adult-only outings. If your own needs for catching the "big one" or collecting gallons of blueberries or paddling 20 miles in three days are met, you will be more patient when you teach your child.

Have the wisdom not to "push." Remember that at some time the child may lose interest in your special skill—be it backpacking, fishing, skiing, whatever. Let go. The child may return later when pressure is not so strong or when interests switch again. It is counterproductive for you to insist on companionship when your child really does not want to go along with you.

Gradually increase the intensity of your outings to suit the child's changing desires. Before you know it, you may be puffing and panting to keep up with the skills and the stamina of your child.

Did You Know?
Rachel Carson
Shared Her Sense of Wonder

Rachel Carson was a marine biologist. She was capable of naming all the plants and animals that she and her nephew Roger discovered as they explored the Maine coast. She chose instead to go "through the woods in the spirit of two friends on an expedition of exciting discovery."

_. . . a sense
of wonder
so indestructible
that
it would last
throughout life. . . ._

Rachel Carson

Carson wrote about her years of exploring the coast with Roger in _The Sense of Wonder,_ a classic work describing the companionship between an adult and a child as they explore the beauty and intricacy of the natural world.

Carson wrote about watching the full moon rise, not worrying about lost sleep. "I think . . . the memory of such a scene, photographed year after year by his child's mind, would mean more to him in manhood than the sleep he was losing."

Rather than direct their walks together, Carson often let Roger's curiosity guide them. She considered the fresh view of a child awe-inspiring:

> If I had influence with the good fairy who is supposed to preside over the christening of all children, I should ask that her gift to each child in the world be a sense of wonder so indestructible that it would last throughout life, as an unfailing antidote against the boredom and disenchantments of later years. . . .

Carson felt the role of a special adult in a child's life was to keep alive that sense of wonder simply by sharing it with the child. She did not believe that an adult needed any particular skills or knowledge to foster that sense of wonder in a child. "I sincerely believe that for the child, and for the parent seeking to guide him, it is not half so important to know as to feel."

Carson's challenge to adults is to look at the stars, listen to the wind, feel the rain and ponder the mysteries of migration.

> Exploring nature with your child is largely a matter of becoming receptive to what lies all around you. It is learning again to use your eyes, ears, nostrils and finger-tips, opening up the disused channels of sensory impression.

She concludes her pictorial essay with a promise:

> Those who contemplate the beauty of the earth find
> reserves of strength that will endure as long as life lasts.
> . . . There is something infinitely healing in the repeated
> refrains of nature—the assurance that dawn comes after
> night, and spring after the winter.

It is not
half so important
to know
as
to feel.

Rachel Carson

Other Ideas
For Teaching a Child a Favorite Skill

1. Identify one fruiting plant, such as the blackberry. Plan an outing to pick the fruit when it is ripe. Freeze what you do not eat, or air-express a pie to the authors of this book!

2. Read about an endangered species. Visit the animal in a zoo or nature preserve.

3. After a snowfall or rain, track a deer or other mammal or a bird. Take along plaster of paris and practice making casts of the animal's footprints.

4. Challenge a group of friends and family members to a wildlife photo contest. Your objective may be to get photographs of the most mammals in one day or to collect water related photos. Be creative. Make up goals and rules of your own.

5. Plan a birthday party to include a scavenger hunt in a park. Include hints about the natural setting, such as "the next clue will be found at the base of the tallest white pine."

6. Map the movement of the Big Dipper through the course of an entire night. Teenagers, especially, will enjoy the challenge—and the opportunity to stay up all night!

7. Study the behavior of birds by maintaining a bird feeding station. Closely observe and keep a log of the behavior of one bird species. Compare the behavior to that of another species.

8. On a family camping trip teach kids about building fires, cooking outdoors and setting up campsites. Give them sole responsibility for making one meal, or for selecting a site and setting up camp.

9. Using pungent plants like mint or sweet fern, design a ten-yard trail for a "nose hike." Blindfold the participants and start them out on their bellies. See if they can sniff their way to the end.

10. Plan a three-generational canoe trip. Follow old routes of your youth or historic pathways of fur traders and explorers.

11. Set aside a section of a flower or vegetable garden. Have your child plant a pumpkin for use as a Halloween jack-o-lantern.

12. Blindfold someone. Then lead the blindfolded person through the woods in a spirit of discovery—feeling, smelling and listening.

Resources

The Sense of Wonder by Rachel Carson. New York: Harper & Row, 1956.

The Life of the Seashore by William Amos. New York: Mc Graw-Hill Book Co., 1966.

The Life of Rivers and Streams by Robert Usinger. New York: McGraw-Hill Book Co., 1967.

A Basic Guide to Fishing: For Freshwater Anglers of All Ages by David Lee. Englewood Cliffs, NJ: Prentice Hall, 1983.

Tom Brown's Field Guide to Nature and Survival for Children by Tom Brown. New York: Berkley Books, 1989.

The Bird Feeder Book: An Easy Guide for Attracting, Identifying and Understanding Your Feeder Birds by Donald and Lillian Stokes. Boston: Little, Brown and Company, 1987.

How to Attract Birds edited by Ken Burke. San Francisco: Ortho Books, 1983.

A Field Guide to Animal Tracks by Olaus J. Murie. Boston: Houghton Mifflin Co., 1974.

Be Expert with Map and Compass: The Orienteering Handbook by Bjorn Kjellstrom. New York: Charles Scribner's Sons, 1976.

Starting Small in the Wilderness (a parents guide to backcountry adventure with children) by Marlyn Doan. San Francisco: Sierra Club Books, 1979

Let's Grow: 72 Gardening Adventures for Children by Linda Tilgner. Pownal, VT: Storey Communications, Inc., 1988.

Exploration
is a journey
that can
lead
in many
directions.

6. In the Arms of the Cottonwood

Exploration implies moving from one place to the next, looking at new sights and sounds, learning new skills and meeting new people.

Exploration can also mean looking in depth at one place—investigating the connections that make the place dynamic, unique and beautiful. Awareness of the sights, sounds and smells around you can be enhanced by sitting quietly in one place.

In this story, Joe silently explores the subtle beauty of a small woodlot from his deer stand. In the process, he discovers deep connections with the earth, the past and his inner self.

In the Arms of the Cottonwood: The Story

The pre-dawn sky was pitch black. Silent. Cold. Joe carefully stepped over the fence that separated barnyard from woodlot. He knew the trail by heart. He stepped Indian fashion, without making a sound.

New snow had fallen during the night. It softened his steps as he quietly passed the old juniper. He stepped over the rotting elm, a victim of the big wind the summer before last. Now it lay asleep beneath the new blanket of white.

Joe stopped. A muffled "whish" swept in front of him. The great horned owl was overhead, returning to roost in the gnarled branches of the old cottonwood after a night of silent hunting. As Joe stood quietly, soft flakes of snow brushing his eyelashes, he felt a partnership with this owl. He had seen it often on other nights. For the rest of the day, Joe would take up where the owl had finished, the day shift replacing the night shift in the hunting factories of this South Dakota woodlot.

Held captive in the suspended silence that preceeds the dawn, Joe was reluctant to move. Yet he knew he must.

As he moved in toward the old cottonwood and scrambled up onto its branches, the great raptor gave over its perch and winged into the darkness without a sound. He was at home there. The tree provided a comfortable resting place from which to watch dawn's first light.

Earlier, when the maples first hinted of the autumn drawing near, Joe had spent days looking for "his tree." He had explored this 10 acres of prairie shelterbelt from corner to corner. Mentally, he had mapped the myriad trails that crisscrossed the half-mile long woodlot, discovering the paths, feeding grounds and signs of its wildlife citizens—the cottontail, squirrel, fox, chickadee and the whitetail deer.

He had explored tree after tree—trying to find the perfect perch—one that offered just the right mix of shelter, safety and, most important, the hunter's vantage point.

During the course of the fall, his perspective changed. He selected and tested tree after tree until he found Grandmother Cottonwood. Once in her loft, he could look down into a tiny meadow which he hoped would be the path of a whitetail en route to the cornfield and the slough.

Now Joe sat and listened. The stars faded as morning illuminated the small opening. Soon, he knew, the early risers would enter the stage below. First there would be a crescendo of song from the chickadees, nuthatches and bluejays. Then the crow would awaken and stretch before day's first flight. Later the cottontail and squirrel would enter, each dancing their own ballet steps to the whispers of wind and the chattering of chickadee-dee-dee.

As the first chorus broke the translucent gray, a gentle breeze whisked fluffy snow from the branches overhead. The flakes drifted slowly onto Joe's arms and the old rifle cradled in them. He sat silently, immersed in the moment.

His thoughts drifted like the snowflakes. Dancers of the past emerged as he thought of the rifle and then of his dad. Joe remembered the boyhood hunts with his father and his brothers—scampering through crispy oak leaves in pursuit of the squirrel.

As a teenager, he had enjoyed deer hunting with his father in the northwoods of Wisconsin near the Flambeau River. At dusk, after a full day of hunting, he especially liked walking alone with his father along the quiet trail. They shared what they had seen and the areas they had explored during the day. Crossing the beaver ponds, ·they walked toward the old hunting cabin, its lantern shining through the window and the scent of pine in the smoke drawing them home. In those moments, they were united, caught in the spirit of the day and at peace.

During such walks, Joe often wondered what spell had overcome them. Everything felt right and blessed. While Joe had spent most of the day actively exploring the tamarack swamps and the beaver ponds, his dad had been quietly sitting near the big maple on a ridge overlooking the stream below—waiting, he said, for the buck to come to him.

Occasionally, Joe tried to sit and wait, but the minutes weighed like years. He always got itchy to hike and track. As they walked together in the dusk at the end of day, Joe felt that the peace and tranquility that shone in his dad's eyes was somehow connected to the silent hours he had spent alone on the maple ridge.

Joe's mind returned from his dad's maple ridge to the cottonwood of the present. Above Joe a nuthatch crept down the trunk, poking its bill into every crack. Soon another alighted, carrying a sunflower seed. The bird stuck the seed into the bark, saving it for another day. Joe remembered how surprised he was the first time he discovered all the sunflower seeds in this pantry. He mused, thinking that he fed the birds and the birds, in turn, fed him with food for thought on this cold November morning.

A noisy approach brought Joe to attention. His heart beat loudly. He adjusted his hold on the old rifle. His mind focused on the whitetail that might emerge from the thicket to the west. Could this be the moment he had waited for all season, first with bow and arrow and now with rifle?

Several times he had seen the big buck, wary and elusive, always aware of Joe before Joe was aware of him. All fall it had been a game of hide and seek. Tracks told Joe of the buck's movements. Lately there had been telltale rubbings on saplings as the buck polished his antlers and prepared for the rut. This buck had also scraped clear small areas in the woodland to leave his scent for does passing by.

During the past few months, Joe had learned much about this buck—for each buck was different. As Joe approached the tree in the twilight, he often heard the buck snort, indicating that once again it had discovered his presence even before he climbed the tree. Still Joe would climb up, aware that the morning would probably not bring the buck across his path that day. He anticipated other things he might discover as he listened quietly in the branches, watching over this small clearing in the woods.

The noise that alerted Joe this time signaled only the activity of a big fox squirrel digging among the leafy debris. It stepped out of its nest of leaves high in the few oaks that still graced this hundred-year-old stand of trees, planted by a homesteader long ago.

A tiny bird flitted onto a branch, inches from Joe's face. Above its sharp bill was a striking cap of yellow. It was the golden-crowned kinglet, which Joe had often seen high in his tree. For three years he had explored this little shelterbelt and had cataloged the birds. Still, the only time he ever saw the kinglet was when he sat quietly in the branches of the old cottonwood.

As he waited, Joe let himself explore the deeper realms of mystery within. He immersed himself into a spell, fashioned by the wind and wings of time. His mind drifted from its search for the whitetail to thoughts of other days, other places, other people.

Earlier he had found his mind drawn to daily concerns and worries. Gradually, as he patiently watched and waited, he became increasingly relaxed and content.

Following this meditative path, his perspective changed. Sitting in the cottonwood the meaning of his father's message blew down from the maple ridge along the Flambeau. Listen. Listen. Listen. In the spell of the dawn, the past and the future merged, and the present became golden.

Activity

Purpose
To explore in depth one place, or one natural object, by sitting quietly and observing for a long period of time.

Age/Number/Setting
Any place outdoors—a canyon, a rock on a lakeshore, a woodlot. Alternatively, you can focus on any natural object outdoors—an ant, a frog, a mouse, a cactus. This type of exploration is best done alone. Youngsters may need or want a parent or adult watching carefully nearby.

Materials
No equipment other than proper clothing is necessary.

How-To   Prepare yourself. Create a quiet, thoughtful focus with questions. "What is the smallest and most interesting creature around here? What do you know about it? How could you learn more?" Or, "If you wanted to quietly sit and watch for animals where would you sit? Why? What would you watch for?"

Allow ample time to explore. A preschooler's patience may be about 15 minutes. An eight-year-old may be able to concentrate for an hour. An adult may need several hours to thoroughly investigate a natural object. As the fisherman on the edge of a pool or a hunter in a deer stand knows, patience is the key.

Pick a specific area or object to watch. Find a comfortable place to 'sit and wait. Look at the shapes and colors of trees, rocks and clouds. Study the details of wood patterns or sand grains. On some days waiting will result in quick rewards like sighting of a red fox or colorful birds, or seeing something old in a fascinating new way. On other days the results may be more subtle, like finding a tranquil moment in a busy week, but its still always rewarding.

Quiet listening can result in a meditative experience and bring restful sleep. If you feel restless, instead of succumbing to the impulse to get up and wander, patiently refocus on your chosen object or place. Focus and refocus. Eventually your breathing will become slower, and you'll begin to relax. Once in this relaxed state you will see things in new ways. You will better understand and accept yourself and your relationship to others and the world.

Afterward share the results of your exploration. Encourage a child to share what he or she did, observed or felt. If the activity involved a group of individuals exploring on their own, reconvene and share observations and thoughts. If the activity was done as a solo, record your impressions in a journal.

The magic of
ordinary nature—
the song of
chickadees,
the croak of frogs,
the rustle of
oak leaves

Did You Know?
You Can Explore By
Staying In One Place

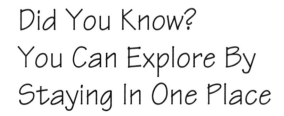

Aldo Leopold was a "one place" explorer *par excellence.* As a naturalist, Leopold reveled in the magic of ordinary nature—the song of chickadees, the croak of frogs, the rustle of oak leaves that he enjoyed on his farm along the Wisconsin River.

Leopold loved this retreat in the sandy country of central Wisconsin. On weekends he and his family explored the banks of the river, walked the eroded hillsides and crept through the tall marsh grass. On windy November days he listened for the ancient rhythmic songs of the geese heading south:

> Out of the clouds I hear a faint bark, as of a faraway dog. It is strange how the world cocks its ears at this sound, wondering. Soon it is louder: the honk of geese, invisible, but coming on.

> The flock emerges from the low clouds, a tattered banner of birds, dipping and rising, blown up and blown down, blown together and blown apart, but advancing, the wind wrestling lovingly with each winnowing wing.

In *A Sand County Almanac,* Leopold portrayed the beauty and seasonal dynamics of this special place. Through his many years at "The Shack" he listened for the wind in autumn, felt the blizzard in winter and smelled wild flowers in spring. He watched chickadees forage for seed and fox catch grouse. He observed nature carefully, learning in turn the rhythmic laws of life in the wild. In the process of thoroughly exploring the fields, marshes and woods surrounding him, Leopold had time to think, to reflect and to discover. Through the pages of his *Almanac*, he shared insights gained and lessons learned.

> It seems likely that weather is the only killer so devoid of both humor and dimension as to kill a chickadee. I suspect that in the chickadee Sunday School two mortal sins are taught: thou shalt not venture into windy places in winter, thou shalt not get wet before a blizzard.

Today Leopold stands as a prophet in the pages of conservation history and environmental ethics. His journey as a visionary naturalist started early. His childhood days were spent exploring the Mississippi River backwaters of Iowa and sharing his father's love of hunting and nature exploration. As a forester in the Gila National Forest of New Mexico, he changed his theories of production forestry and predator control to fit ecological realities. He was a pioneer in scientific wildlife management and wrote the textbook on the subject. As an advocate for wilderness, he challenged current thinking.

Throughout his life, Leopold was an astute observer—he watched carefully and recorded his findings. During his walks along the Wisconsin River, he dreamed of the earth and of ways to restore its beauty. Along this river he also synthesized discoveries made during his years of exploring into a new way of thinking about humanity and the earth.

> We abuse land because we regard it as a commodity belonging to us. When we see land as a community to which we belong, we may begin to use it with love and respect. . . . That land is a community is the basic concept of ecology, but that land is to be loved and respected is an extension of ethics.

Aldo Leopold
dreamed
of the earth
and
ways to restore
its beauty.

Other Ideas
For Exploring One Place or Object in Depth

1. Take a micro-hike along a three- to five-foot strand of string. Lay the string out over an interesting spot of ground. With a magnifying glass in hand, set out in the spirit of thinking small and looking for tiny intricacies—veins of leaves, flower pollen, insect trails on rotting logs.

2. Walk until you find a tree with a comfortable place to lie down near it. Sit or lie down facing the tree with your feet on the trunk. What do you see? How are you like the tree? Unlike the tree? What other creatures use the tree? What does the tree say to you? This kind of contemplation can also be done looking at a lake, a cliff, a plant, a bird or an animal.

3. Raise a peanut, bean or sunflower from seed. Record growth measurements periodically.

4. Build a tree fort with your child. Share a sunrise breakfast in it. Note all the creatures you see and hear.

5. Study the natural or cultural history of an area before visiting it. Or, read a novel about the area. Examples: James Michener's *Centennial,* Laura Ingalls Wilder's *Little House on the Prairie.*

6. Join The Nature Conservancy or another organization dedicated to preserving unique natural habitats and go on organized outings.

7. Photograph one place through each of the seasons, and from year to year.

8. Using a tape recorder, tape a night sound. Listen carefully to it. Try to identify it as a frog, owl, insect, etc. Also, try to identify what the creature is communicating. Find a naturalist who can confirm or correct your identification.

9. Choose a brief period of time and mimic the activities of your cat or dog. Use discretion—you may not want to eat cat food!

10. Find an accessible fire tower and climb it. Get permission if necessary, and use caution. Like a bird, view the world from above.

11. Keep a notebook on the natural changes that occur where you live—the first spring rain, the migration of birds, the first leaves out, the frogs or crickets talking, changing colors in the fall, bicycles being put away for the winter.

12. Toss a brick or other small object into a lake. Dive to retrieve it again and again as you explore the underwater world.

Resources

A Sand County Almanac by Aldo Leopold. San Francisco: Sierra Club/Ballantine Books, 1970.

Aldo Leopold: His Life and Works by Curt Meine. Madison, WI: The University of Wisconsin Press, 1988.

The Dream of the Earth by Thomas Berry. New York: Doubleday Books, 1989.

Wild Season by Allan Eckert. New York: Bantam Books, 1967.

One Day on Beetle Rock by Sally Carrighar. New York: Ballantine Books, 1944.

Ceremonial Time by John H. Mitchell. New York: Warner Books, 1984.

The View from the Oak by Judith and Herbert Kohl. New York: Charles Scribner's Sons, 1977.

Whitetail Country: The Photographic Life History of Whitetail Deer by Daniel Cox. Wautoma, WI: Willow Creek Press, 1988.

The Giving Tree by Shel Silverstein. New York: Harper & Row, Inc., 1964.

Quiet by Peter Parnell. New York: Morrow Junior Books, 1989.

Exploration
is a journey
that can
lead
in many
directions.

7. Journey Into the Past

Earlier landscapes and lifestyles can be explored through conversations or photographs. Visits with grandparents, senior relatives or community elders are a great way to become better acquainted with a place. Old photo albums provide a priceless journey into the past.

The following story illustrates Joe's connection to the central Wisconsin farm that his great grandparents first cleared and homesteaded. Through four generations the farm has bonded this family together.

In the activity you will be invited to explore your family's roots and your connections to the land.

Journey Into the Past: The Story

The sweet smell of newly cut hay drifted into the car window reminding Joe of earlier rides to Grandma and Grandpa's farm.

The road wound its way through the pines and oaks near the Wisconsin River and then turned north toward pastures and cornfields. Large red barns and square white farmhouses contrasted brightly with the green of hayfields and the yellow of ripening oats. The black, white and brown of Holstein and Guernsey cows added more color to the landscape.

Joe remembered Sunday afternoons when his family piled into the old Dodge to go to Grandma's. Joe loved to sing "Home on the Range." Through leaps of a five-year-old's imagination, the roadside cows looked like the "deer and the antelope" of the song. Family sing-alongs helped shorten the hour ride. Those were great Sundays—a time to play with cousins, hear stories from uncles, eat Grandma's cookies and pies and sit on Grandpa's lap as he relaxed in the rocking chair beside the wood-burning stove. Joe especially liked the evenings when the sounds of polka music and dancing drifted into the yard and pasture. There Joe and his cousins would play hide and seek, watch stars and try to capture the elusive "star bugs" of the night as they fluttered over the newly-cut hayfields.

Joe returned to the present and his car when he heard his mother hum a family lullaby to his three-year-old son, Forest. Joe and his mother talked about planting and harvesting and about changes—births, marriages and deaths—that marked the cadence of this family's hundred-year tie to Wisconsin farm land. Joe was thankful that his grandma still guarded the family hearth. This summer, the family would celebrate her 90th birthday. She was the fragile, golden thread. She tied generations and legends to the land. Joe was glad to be back sharing this rich family legacy with his mother, wife and son.

As they walked up to the porch, Joe could see that his grandma's pink roses were blooming. The foursome stopped to enjoy the fragrance. Through the window they could see Grandma next to the stove, fixing supper. She greeted them with kisses and hugs, offering the traditional cookies and cup of coffee that marked the hospitality of this home and this small farming town.

Joe glanced at the religious pictures and photos on the wall, and smelled the aroma of sauerkraut.

A photo of Joe's grandfather, now 10 years deceased, brought back memories of boyhood summers. Along with daily farm chores, Joe had helped Grandpa cut the tall grass at the German cemetery where the family's relatives were buried. Many of the tombstones listed birthplaces in Germany and Switzerland. Watching his Grandpa swing the long hand scythe through the grass—swish, swish, swish—

Joe had imagined what life was like in the Swiss Alps. The farmland surrounding the cemetery told of the century-long effort to tame the Wisconsin woods and bogs and turn them into the likes of the verdant pastures they remembered from Switzerland.

While Joe's grandma, mother and wife prepared supper, Joe took Forest on a tour of the big house. Joe especially liked to climb the open staircase that led to the attic. He had played on the steps as a boy.

The steps creaked as Joe carried Forest toward the attic. He stopped to look at an aging photo on the wall. In it four brothers relaxed, each holding a glass of solid German brew while admiring the new home they had just finished building. There stood this proud, new Wisconsin farm house with its long, white open porch.

"Forest, that's my grandpa," said Joe as he pointed to the young man in the picture leaning against the porch rail. "He's your great-grandpa. He and his brothers helped their dad build this house, the one we're in right now. Grandma says that my grandpa and my great-uncle Joe made this staircase and all the woodwork in the house from just one giant white pine that they cut. I'll show you a picture of the tree later. Before they moved here, there were trees everywhere. They cut them down to make farmland."

Forest peered through the polished pine rails of the staircase. He dashed up the stairs and ran down a long hallway. Joe peeked into the side rooms and finally caught up with Forest.

"This was my room when I spent summers here as a boy," Joe said, leading Forest to the window. Joe remembered open fields with just a few shade trees around the house. He was astonished at the growth of the trees planted during the past 50 years to shelter the house from the winter winds. Now they enfolded the old home, cutting off the view to the pump-house and the big barn where Joe used to play.

Forest was busy looking down the open register in the floor of the bedroom. Joe knelt next to his son and peered through the grate to the floor below. "Look, Forest, there's your great-grandma. She's setting the table for dinner, just like she's done for almost a hundred years. Dinner sure smells good."

The rich aromas of roast beef and sauerkraut drifted through the register, which drew the warm air up from the woodstove below.

Joe closed his eyes and saw the dining room filled with big men—farmers in rough clothes with oat chaff in their hair. The neighbors rested during the midday heat, drinking German beer, eating and laughing. Their wives had joined forces in the hot kitchen. They cooked chicken and dumplings, potatoes and pies on the big black cookstove. Joe imagined again hearing the gigantic threshing machine spin and rumble outside as it chewed up sheaves of oats tossed in by men riding the golden mountain stacked high on the hay wagon. The threshing machine spit out a blizzard of yellow straw and a stream of golden grain.

Joe laughed when he saw Forest dropping pennies down the register. "I liked doing that, too, when I was a kid," he said.

The two walked back into the big hallway. As Joe slowly opened another door, he smelled the distinctive odor of old things—things left and saved. No longer used, yet precious. This room smelled just as it had when he first discovered its mysteries almost 40 years earlier.

Joe picked up Forest and, honoring tradition, tiptoed into the room. In the corner, long hickory skis stood near the dusty shotguns that kept vigil over these remnants of the past. Joe was in his ancestor's domain, a place of spirits, and his grandma was its steward. Joe was thankful for this guardian angel who had safe-guarded these relics and kept alive the memories of the Draxlers and the Martis, two families emigrating from the old country in the mid-1800s.

Under the tapestry of an old curtain lay a special treasure: the box-like trunk commemorating his great-grandfather's trip to America. These words, "M. Marti, Basel-Harve (Switzerland)—New York-Wisconsin-Monroe," traced the journey from the high Alps of Switzerland to the woods and farmlands of Auburndale, Wisconsin.

Joe removed the curtain and slowly raised the lid. Inside lay holy vestiges of the past. As he picked up the German Bible, he again heard Grandma's dialect as she prayed for the good life —rain, good crops and happy children. Beside the book lay a cloth richly decorated with embroidery and crochet. The embroidery, some of Joe's great-grandmother's, was accented with the same pink roses his grandmother was so fond of—both on cloth and in the garden. In the past 10 years, Grandma had lovingly embroidered a set of pillowcases for each of her 77 grandchildren. Joe's set of pillowcases rested in another trunk—a trunk full of treasures connecting him to his past and his family.

Forest reached into the trunk and picked up a picture. He turned it over and handed it to Joe. Together they gazed at the print, as crisp as the day its image was developed. It was the same photo they had seen earlier on the wall, only smaller. Joe's great-uncle Joe had taken this and hundreds of other photos of the Draxler-Marti clan and the logging camps, farms and community events of the late 1800s.

The door creaked open and toes tapped on the dusty wooden floor. It was Joe's mom. She looked at the photo with Joe and then, looking at Forest, pointed to the man leaning against the porch rail. "That's my daddy, your great-grandpa," she said. "He helped his dad and brothers build this house."

She reached for another photo. In the picture stood two lumberjacks with their saw half through a gigantic pine. "That's my grandpa and Uncle Joe. That's the tree they cut down to build this house." Forest picked up another photo and handed it to his grandma. The stories of past generations were repeated once again for a new generation.

Joe thought of the woman downstairs from whom he first heard, as a boy, the story of the woods that begot the tree, the tree that was transformed into the house and the land that supported the family.

The three were brought from their reflections by footsteps on the pine staircase. "Come and eat. The sauerkraut is getting cold," rang Grandma's German voice. "And bring them old pictures down. We can look at them again after supper."

Activity

Purpose
To explore your family's heritage and connection to the natural world through the use of stories and photographs.

Age/Number/Setting
Family members of all ages can participate. Crucial to this activity are the memories, records and photos of older generations. The best setting is at an older relative's home, where family photos and other heirlooms may spark questions and inspire lively discussions.

Materials
Initially all you need is the time to visit and the patience to listen. Later, depending on your objectives, notebooks, tape recorders and cameras can help record memories of past events.

How-To
Start with a small gathering of immediate family members. Encourage older members of the family to share memories from their childhood by asking about special outings, visits and vacations. "What was your favorite vacation as a child? How did you travel? What was the country like? What did you do? Who did you visit?"

Explore the daily events of earlier times by asking where your older relatives lived as children, whether the setting was urban or rural, where they went to school, what they did before and after school. Ask them to describe how the land has changed over the years, how farming, industry and commerce have affected the land. How were their families employed and what roles did they play in the changing landscape?

Take an album along to the gathering to help stimulate the discussion. Go beyond the identification of people and their relationships. View the photos carefully for evidence of natural surroundings and lifestyles.

If appropriate, move to other locations—the attic, the barn, the yard, the garden, or the countryside—to expand the discussion. Encourage the older relatives to show special heirlooms and share their memories.

As a family, write a letter or make a special scrapbook or album of the day's events. Have all family members contribute something they learned and liked. Share the letters or albums with others who participated. Someday, the letters and albums might be considered heirlooms by later generations.

Did You Know?
Searching for Roots
Is a National Pastime

A hunger
for information
once passed from
generation
to
generation
by oral tradition.

In 1966, a high school English teacher in the Appalachian Mountains of northeast Georgia helped his students develop a quarterly magazine containing articles drawn from the local residents. The students interviewed their grandparents and elders.

They documented with tape recorders and cameras such nearly forgotten skills as planting by the signs of the zodiac, hide tanning, spinning and weaving. They were coached and inspired by their teacher, Elliott Wigginton, to produce *Foxfire*.

In its initial years, the project was small and obscure. And then, like its name sake—a mushroom that glows in the dark—it began to illuminate the minds and hearts of millions. The *Foxfire* books, all eight volumes, have reawakened a hunger for information once passed from generation to generation by oral tradition. The books sparked a nationwide interest in rural lifestyles, in exploring ways of living with the land and in being taught by our elders.

Oral tradition is a way for one generation to teach another. In the past, it has been the predominant way to pass on skills, community values and lifestyles. Native Americans and immigrants also taught their children by working side-by-side. Parents and grandparents taught children as they tended to the daily chores of making a living with the land. Communities gathered for seasonal celebrations of syruping, planting, harvesting and thanksgiving.

The *Foxfire* project was a reconnection with that oral tradition. Students traveled throughout their rural communities to learn skills and hear stories from the old people. Folklore, the study of skills and traditions of a culture, returned to the common people. Riddles, games, rites of passage, earth festivals, weather lore, medicine, architecture, legends, preservation of food, tools and agricultural techniques emerged from this exploration of rural neighborhoods, towns and regions.

Children are naturally drawn to grandparents and other elders. They sense that elders often have the time and patience to explore with them, as well as experience and knowledge that they enjoy sharing. All the participants in this traditional learning process gain awareness of being part of a larger procession of people.

> Children are naturally drawn to grandparents and other elders.

Other Ideas
For Finding Your Roots to the Land

1. Write a history of the land you live on. Include how the land has been used, types of plants and animals that have inhabited it, and who has lived on it.

2. Graft the branch of an apple tree or other fruit tree from your childhood homestead onto a compatible tree in your present surroundings.

3. Take a core sample of a tree, or find a downed tree and cut a section. By counting the rings, you'll find out how old the tree is. On a sheet of paper, make a timeline for the tree's life. Coordinate it with your family's history.

4. Celebrate the summer solstice as your ancestors or the people who settled your region would have.

5. Find an old-time gardener in your community and ask when some of the trees were planted.

6. Find pictures of your old home, park or school. Study the vegetation in the photo. Visit the site and note any changes.

7. Make a cabin, packsack, chair or other object with your grandparents' old-time tools.

8. Describe the journey of immigrants in your family, paying special attention to land uses (like farming or logging or fishing) that affected their decision to immigrate.

9. With grandparents or older neighbors, return to a favorite place of their youth—a park, a fishing stream, a woodlot. Talk about why it was special and what they did there.

10. Write a letter to a special child in your life about the beauty of your world. Share with her or him things you would like to pass on to the next generation.

Resources

The Foxfire Books edited by Elliot Wigginton. New York: Anchor Books, Doubleday and Co., 1972-87.

A River Runs Through It by Norman McLean. Chicago: University of Chicago Press, 1976.

Our Vanishing Landscape by Eric Sloane. New York: Ballantine Books, 1955.

Shoots: A Guide to Your Family's Photographic Heritage by Thomas L. Daview. Danbury, CT: Addison House, 1967.

Photos From Wisconsin's Past by Malcolm Rosholt. Rosholt, WI: Rosholt House, 1986.

Roots for Kids: A Geneology Guide for Young People by Susan Provost Beller. Crozet, VA: Betterway Publications, 1989.

How to Trace Your Family History by Bill B. Linder. New York: Everest House Publishers, 1978.

Kids America by Steven Carney. New York: Workman Publishing, 1978.

Little House on the Prairie (and other books) by Laura Ingalls Wilder. New York: Harper & Row, 1935.

Seed Savers Exchange: The First Ten Years 1975-1985 edited by Kent Whealy and Arilys Adelmann. Decorah, IA: Seed Savers Publications, 1986. (Membership supported exchange of heirloom seeds and plants) Rural Route 3, Box 239, Decorah, Iowa 52101.

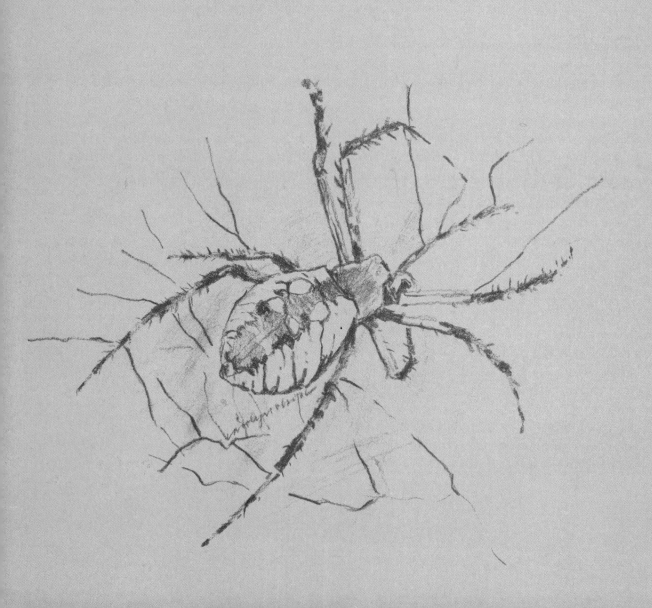

Have you ever encountered the attitude that there are no more unique challenges, no more frontiers to cross, nothing new to invent—the assumption that all important discoveries have already been made? It's an attitude that breeds disinterest and lethargy about the wonder of our world.

We believe that there is no end to discovery. An infinite number of discoveries still remain. Discoveries are made every day, everywhere. They are made by everyone who is actively exploring the natural world.

In some now-forgotten biology class you may have learned how spiders incubate their eggs. But that fact will not be fully relevant or profound until you actually see it for the first time and experience for yourself the wonder of that discovery. In a moment of awareness, you will make the connection to other experiences, other ideas, other pieces of information—and your world will expand.

Discoveries are a natural outgrowth of exploration, but the moment of awareness distinguishes discovery from exploration. Each discovery contributes to your development as an individual. Each has an influence on who you are. You are the sum of all your discoveries. They shape you, change you, enable you to grow and see your world anew.

Moments of discovery open our eyes to higher truths or wider perspectives. A magnificent sunset over a lake may lead us to recognize the vastness of the universe. A newborn fawn may help us understand the uniqueness and interdependence of all living beings.

Discoveries are associated with a strong impulse to share. The bridge between individuals, cultures and generations is fostered by the sharing of discoveries. We encourage you to share your discoveries with others. In doing so, we believe you not only sustain your own sense of wonder, but you form a network—like a spider's web—between you and your friends.

DISCOVERY

8. Spring's Sweet Flow

When the grass peeks out from the edges of snowbanks and the sun finally rises before six in the morning, the eternal hope of spring rises once again in the hearts of Northerners. This is the season of melt.

Best yet, this is the season of maple syruping. In mid-March, when temperatures drop below freezing at night but rise into the high 30s or 40s during the day, a special sweet begins to flow.

The skills acquired in this activity lead you to a treat and to the magic of spring. This activity is an example of how you can read about a skill and lead your family into it.

Spring's Sweet Flow: The Story

"Hey, Mom!" yelled three-year-old Sally. "Look at me!"

She slid on her snowpants down the little incline, just missing a small maple tree. She stopped when she plowed into her six-year-old brother.

The two of them laughed and giggled and urged Ann to follow.

With buckets and spouts balanced on her lap, Ann slid down to join them. However, Dave, carrying the hand drill and hammer, opted for the more cautious but laborious route of pushing steps into the crusty snow. They were in their family "sugarbush," a one-acre woodlot across the street from their home.

"This one is my tree," said Sally.

"That's not a maple tree," said Brian with authority. "Mom marked the maple trees. Only maple trees make syrup."

"Not entirely true, Brian," said Dave. "Other trees can make syrup but not as well as maples. How many kinds of trees are around here?"

Brian and Sally easily identified the white-barked birch trees. Dave also pointed out an aspen, an oak and a chokecherry.

In an hour the family had eight trees tapped. Brian had partially drilled one tree. Sally's help had taken the form of sampling the sweet, clear liquid that came from each tree.

Then it was time to do some exploring. Soon the foursome came to a tree with a large hollow place in the base. Both kids could stand up inside the hollow.

Ann peered up inside, "Look, I can see light! This tree must be hollow clear up to that hole by the big branch."

"Does this tree make sap?" asked Dave.

"No!" was the unanimous consent.

"Don't be so sure," Dave said. "Can you see any buds at the ends of the branches?" The children stepped back from the tree and determined that the tree really was alive because it had branches with buds. All trees that are alive send sap to the tips of the branches in the spring. That sap is food for the leaves to grow.

"Do you think anything uses this hollow for a house?" asked Dave.

"A bear!" said Brian.

"Maybe. What else?" persisted Dave.

Not to be outdone, Sally answered, "A squirrel."

"Good thinking, Sally," said Ann. "How about something bigger?"

"We give up, you tell us," said Brian.

"I don't know for sure," said Ann. "I never noticed this hole before, but I'll guess a raccoon. Can we find any tracks or fur that might tell us?"

There was no evidence to confirm any of their guesses, but their search led them to the dainty tracks of a mouse.

On some days the trips to the sugarbush were a chore. When the snow turned to mush, it meant wet snowpants and hard walking. When it was overcast, windy and snowy, the cold hike was not rewarded with much sap in the buckets. Or even worse, they discovered that the buckets had blown down, spilling the precious liquid.

But there were so many days with special memories. One day, when Dave had gone to work early and Brian was content to play in the house by himself, Ann and Sally ventured out with the spare bucket. And a cup.

"I brought a cup for you to drink sap out of," Ann said. The first tap bucket was nearly full. Ann poured it into the five-gallon plastic pail in front of Sally and gave her a drink.

Then there was the morning they had to redrill a hole because it wasn't producing much sap. "Mom, does it hurt the tree to get drilled?" asked Brian.

"What do you think?" asked Ann.

"Yeah, I think it would hurt," he answered.

"We try to be careful to drill only the holes we need," said Ann. "The trees we tap still make pretty leaves, don't they?"

"Yeah."

"That tells us that we are not taking away all of the tree's sap, that they still have enough left to make leaves. Look at this scar on the tree," Ann said pointing to the tree she was drilling.

Brian edged closed and found the round mark Ann was pointing to.

"That's where we put the tap last year," he said confidently.

"Right!" answered Ann. "Does it look like it hurt the tree any more than a scab you might get on your arm from a little cut?"

"No."

"I'm really glad you are thinking about what is good for the tree," said Ann. "The tree is giving us food. We must give a gift in return, the gift of respect and care."

Activity

Purpose	To collect and prepare maple syrup. To discover the magic of early spring.
Age/Number/Setting	People of all ages can participate. This is written as a family activity. The setting can be any maple woods in the northern tier of states.
Materials	Ice cream buckets or plastic gallon milk jugs, hand drill with a 5/8-inch bit, hammer, spiles (spouts for the trees), canning jars.

How-To   It is far easier to identify maple trees in the fall than in late winter. Mark their location by drawing a map, tagging or flagging the trees. If you do not own any maple trees, don't let that deter you. Many people, if asked, are willing to share their trees. And sap can also be gathered and cooked quite successfully from other trees, most notably birch and box elder. Their syrup is delicious.

Gather materials. By March, you should have collected as many ice cream buckets or milk jugs as you have marked trees. For a first-time operation a half dozen trees is a good number. You will get enough syrup to feel that the effort is worthwhile, but the boiling-down procedure will not seem so drawn out. Spiles or spouts for the trees can be purchased for less than a dollar from hardware or seed and feed stores. Or follow the advice of Laura Ingalls Wilder in her chapter on maple syruping in *Little House in the Big Woods* and make the spouts of sumac branches.

Keep a daily record of signs that herald the change from winter to spring. Swelling buds, running water, melting icicles, kids riding bicycles and returning birds are all clues that syruping time is near.

When daily temperatures fluctuate from the 20s at night to the 40s during the day, it's time to tap the trees. Shallow borings yield better quality, less quantity. Holes deeper than three inches can damage the tree. The tap hole should be at a slight angle so sap will drip out.

Visit the trees daily. When the sap is really flowing, you can collect more than a gallon a day per tap from each tree. Make each excursion to collect sap an adventure in outdoor exploration.

After returning from the woods, pour the sap into a larger container, straining it through a clean cotton cloth.

Begin the boil-down process as soon as possible. If it is cool outside, the sugary sap can be stored there for a week. However, if you must store the sap indoors, keep in mind that it will begin to grow mold after several days.

Sap from the tree is 90 to 99 percent water. Nearly all of the water must be boiled off to get to the maple syrup. The most ideal boil-down is over a wood fire or campstove outdoors. This way you avoid the accumulation of too much water vapor in your house. With care, though, boiling can be done indoors. Depending on the sugar content of the trees, it will take 20 to 40 gallons of sap to make one gallon of syrup. That means a *lot* of boiling. *Caution. Watch your boiling sap. A boil-over is a giant mess.*

How do you tell when the syrup is ready? If you get serious about syruping, invest in a hydrometer, a simple instrument that tells you the percentage of sugar in the syrup. For first-timers the "jelly" test of letting it drip off a metal spoon until the second drop crystalizes works fairly well. Filtering finished syrup through wool felt removes unwanted particles and improves the appearance of the syrup.

The final steps are simple: Pour boiling syrup into sterilized jars, seal, cool and then put them into the refrigerator.

The final product is not like commercial table syrup. Real maple syrup is variable in color and thickness, depending on how it is prepared. It ranges from a thick, dark brown to a thinner, golden product. And the flavor? Well, you've got to taste it to believe it! Invite the neighbors over for a pancake breakfast. Give syrup away as a Christmas present. Try out some recipes in *The Little House Cookbook* by Barbara Walker.

Did You Know?
Maple Syruping
Is an Ancient Art

For centuries,
Indians
have used the sap
from the maple
as a refreshing
drink
or have processed it
into
syrup and candy.

Native Americans have been collecting sap for centuries. From the Algonquin and Iroquois of the northeast to the Huron and Chippewa of the Great Lakes, Indians have used the sap from the maple as a refreshing drink or have processed it into syrup or candy. The Menominee used maple sugar and syrup as a seasoning, often in place of salt. For some, like the Huron, maple syrup was the sole food in times of famine. For the Chippewa, maple products constituted about one-twelfth of their annual diet.

Native Americans cut small wedges into trees and set reeds or hollow twigs into the holes. The sap ran into troughs made from elm or basswood. Usually the sap was heated in green birchbark kettles and reduced to syrup. Maple sap items were important for trade with the settlers. Eventually the settlers produced their own, taking advantage of their metal cooking pots.

You can visit a number of historical maple-sugaring sites. Dodge Nature Center or Fort Snelling in St. Paul, or Forest History Center in Grand Rapids, Minnesota; and Fort William in Thunder Bay, Ontario, are some examples. Talk to interpreters there about how sugaring was done by Indians and early settlers.

Today, technology has been applied to maple sugaring. Now only small, backyard operations use buckets that must be emptied individually. Modern operations use gravity flow systems that bring the sap from the trees into a holding tank, where it goes through an osmosis unit to take out impurities and some of the water. Then it is boiled in sterile, stainless-steel vats.

Whether learning about past or present methods of maple syruping, be sure to conduct a taste test. Compare genuine maple syrup to a typical grocery store imitation. Make the testing a family affair.

Other Ideas for Living with the Land

1. Plant fruit trees and berry plants (raspberry, strawberry, currants) in your yard or in a community garden plot. Make your own jam or gather the fruit for pies; or spread out the mashed pulp on a cookie sheet and make fruit leather.

2. Go with a naturalist to find out about edible plants. Gather the foods needed for a complete meal: fish with a stick or hand-tooled hook; gather berries for dessert; make sumac lemonade or an herbal tea for drinks; find tubers and salad greens for the main meal.

3. Pick an early American craft and learn the skill: basketry, rug making, quilting, tanning and leatherwork, making rope or twine, soapmaking and candlemaking. Teach the skill to a friend or child. Give your creations as gifts.

4. Build a debris hut: Use only dead trees and plant materials. Lean a ridgepole the length of your body against a rock or tree. Use other branches and sticks to make the ribs. Cover with forest litter.

5. Collect pine cones. Isolate the seeds, dry them and plant them. Transplant the seedlings into larger containers before you put them outdoors.

6. If you are an angler, extend your skills and learn to fish with a simple line and hook and natural bait. If you're a hunter, try your skills at bow-and-arrow hunting.

7. Practice making fires under many conditions: snow, rain, with little tinder, scarce kindling.

8. Explore an arid environment, seeking a source of water. Imagine you are an animal, such as a coyote, in need of water daily.

Resources

Amateur Sugar Maker by Noel Perrin. Hanover, MA: University Press of New England, 1986.

Maple Syrup Producer's Manual by C.O. Willits and Claude H. Mills. Agriculture Handbook #134. Washington, D.C.: U.S. Government Printing.

Tom Brown's Field Guide to Wild, Edible and Medicinal Plants by Tom Brown. New York: Berkley Books, 1985.

The Kids Nature Book: 365 Indoor/Outdoor Activities and Experiences by Susan Milford. Charlotte, VT: Williamson Publishing, 1989.

The Long Ago Lake: A Child's Book of Nature Lore and Crafts by Marne Wilkins. New York: Charles Scribner's Sons, 1978.

The Little House Cookbook: Frontier Foods from Laura Ingalls Wilder's Classic Stories by Barbara M. Walker. New York: Harper & Row, Publishers, 1979.

Wild Food Cookbook by Francis Hamerstrom. Ames, IA: Iowa State University Press, 1989.

American Indian Food and Lore: 150 Authentic Recipes by Carolyn Niethammer. New York: Macmillan Publishing Co., Inc., 1974.

Fruits and Berries by The American Horticultural Society. Mount Vernon, VA, 1982.

Blueberries For Sal by Robert McCloskey. New York: Viking, 1948.

9. The Gift of Fire

From the flicker of a candle to a roaring blaze, fire has fascinated young and old since the beginning of humankind. Fire has been a tool with many uses; a source of danger and fear; and a provider of comfort, warmth and light. Our distant ancestors saw in fire the mysteries of the supernatural.

Today we continue to be awed and nourished by the warmth of an open fire. Building a campfire can awaken a sense of wonder about the primal forces of nature and strengthen a sense of dependence on the earth.

In this story, students learn the skill of building a campfire and in so doing discover the magic of working together.

The Gift of Fire: The Story

The thermometer read 25 degrees below zero. Eleven college students, new to the Northwoods, huddled around Joe as he crouched in the snow. A blizzard raged around them—dropping the wind chill to 70 below. Joe seemed to be praying over a stack of dead sticks.

Someone asked, "Should we get the marshmallows yet, Joe?" Everyone laughed nervously. The next call was for hot dogs.

Joe had one match per intern. He was convinced that they would be able "to catch at least one fire." The fire-building lesson was important. During the next three months, these 11 interns would be guardians of 5,000 eager elementary and high school students who would spend a week at the Environmental Learning Center in northern Minnesota.

"Well, this is a good start to building a fire," said Joe. "But the best fire is always your own. I'm going to hold on to my one match until you all have gathered kindling and built fires."

He gave each intern a single match and divided the young people into groups of three. Then he raised his arms and said, "Go forth and build us a fire!"

Jim, Sue and Kelly stood dumbfounded in their little group. They looked at one another and the single match each held. They were unsure of their skills in this new environment and were just beginning to know each other.

Finally, Jim took over. He bounded through the snow and yelled to the others. "Come on, let's go! Let's win this contest. I've built fires before. I even won a prize when I was in Boy Scouts."

Remembering Joe's brief lesson, the threesome carefully selected a sheltered site, cleared away the snow and gathered tinder, sticks and branches.

"Start with the aspen leaves; they'll burn every time," said Jim.

Sue suggested they first make a base of larger branches to help keep the tinder dry.

The reality of working with bulky mittens in bitter temperatures added an urgency to their efforts. With all three staring in anticipation at the pile of sticks, Jim said, "That's good enough, I'll light the aspen leaves." However, unlike the leaves of Indian summer these leaves did not burn merrily. They simply smoked. The smoke burned Jim's eyes. He thrust his hand back into his mitten.

"Let me try the pine needles," suggested Sue. "They always flare up!"

They flared up, but the fire-builders had forgotten to put on bigger twigs.

"I'll bet this birch bark starts," Kelly said as he rearranged the tinder. While everyone else jumped around to keep warm, he lit the group's last match. The birch bark took the flame. It snapped and sizzled as it burned the leaves around it, but their hopes flickered and died when the leaves began to smoke again.

"I hope I never get lost up here with you guys," kidded Sue, "We'd really be in trouble!"

Disappointed, the three trudged back to find Joe and the others.

The rest of the interns had already returned to the meeting place—flitting about like chickadees, and stamping their feet to stay warm. They were comparing notes on their respective failures.

Kelly finally spoke for the group, "I still think the birch bark is the trick, but we will need a lot to get the fire started. Let's try it again."

Joe offered his one last match. Together they picked the best site, the driest wood and lots of birch bark.

Joe shouted, "Let's go, Kelly! Start the fire!

I'm freezing to death!"

As they huddled closer around the carefully arranged star-shaped collection of birch bark and twigs, Kelly crouched in the snow and struck the last match. He touched it to a piece of paper-thin birch bark. No one joked. The flickering orange flame slowly grew. It ignited more bark and then some cedar twigs.

With a surge of premature joy, Jim jumped, yelled and accidentally kicked snow on the pile of twigs—a pile that had taken on sacred proportions and holy mysteries. Fear struck the hearts of all as the melting snow hissed. But the candle of birch bark continued to nourish the flame, and this time, in silent awe, all 12 thanked the Great Spirit for "the gift of fire."

Activity

Purpose
To discover the art of fire building and the magic of working together.

Age/Number/Setting
If the primary purpose is to build survival skills and a cooperative spirit, this activity works best with teenagers and adults divided into groups of two to four, in a woodland setting where it is alright to gather combustible materials. Make the task challenging, but not impossible. If the group is skilled, work in winter. If not, try it in warmer, drier weather. With parental guidance the activity can easily be adapted to a family adventure with younger children, in settings from the back yard to the state park.

Materials   One match per individual or an alternative fire starter like a fire drill or flint and steel. *Important:* Be safety conscious. Clear the ground in a circle several feet away from the fire. Bank the circle with earth or stones. Have water or snow nearby to control and extinguish the fire.

How-To   Set the stage for the activity. Tell a story about fire. See "Did You Know" for a legend of how the spirits gave us the gift of fire. Briefly discuss the views of people toward fire—as friend, foe or sacred symbol.

Form groups of two to four. Discuss survival situations such as winter camping, an airplane crash, or a lost hiker. Assign each group the task of building a survival fire—a fire that will provide warmth, water, comfort and companionship. As an added challenge, have each group boil a cup of herbal tea made from a plant they must first gather.

Before sending the group off, review the basic elements needed for a fire—heat, combustible material and oxygen. Make a fire using the group's collective skills and knowledge. Give each person a match and send the teams out. Visit each team. With the exception of the one fire you choose for follow-up activities, have each group properly extinguish its fire.

Once your fire is built, watch it, enjoy its warmth and think reflectively. Talk about the combustibles the fire builders found and discuss how the team members worked together. Encourage the group to develop legends of how the gift of fire was given. If you develop legends individually, provide paper and pencil for all participants to write or to create a sketch, using charcoal from their own fire. Songs and skits could also be encouraged. These follow-up activities can be done indoors when the weather is bad.

Did You Know?
The Legend About a Stolen Fire

Our ancestors saw in fire the mysteries of the supernatural. Sacred rites are filled with the symbolism of fire . . . from the sacrificial fires of Baal and the holy candles of Catholicism to the sacred sun dance and purification rituals of the Sioux Indians.

But where did fire come from? Charles Wood recorded a Nez Perce legend of obtaining fire in *A Book of Indian Tales.*

According to the Cayuses Tribe of the Nez Perce nation, all of the fire in the world was, at one time, inside a volcano (now named Mount Hood on maps). Hon-ea-woat, the Creator and Great Spirit, had given this fire to the Fire Demon. The demon kept the fire from everyone—from all animals and from all men.

The Nez Perce did not need fire at that time, for they had feathers and thick furs. But one autumn, the Nez Perce had a great celebration and took off their animal skins to dance. A great eagle carried away the skins, leaving the people cold and afraid.

Two braves decided to steal fire from the demon of the fire mountain. One disguised himself as a log by covering himself with the bark of trees. Just as he was about to be put in the fire, he jumped up, snatched a piece of fire and ran down the mountain. The braves fled, with the Fire Demon close behind. They ran so fast that they melted the snow as they ran. Their path is marked today by the John Day River.

The Great Spirit was willing for the Nez Perce to have the fire, so he changed all the fire demons into pine trees and one of the braves into a beaver. The beaver then swam across the river of melted snow and spat the fire into a willow log. That is why the

Sacred rites
are filled
with the
symbolism
of fire.

87

willow is one of the woods from which to rub fire. The brave who stole the fire was changed into a woodpecker, which still creeps around trees, tapping with its bill to show that fire is in the wood.

Native people have many legends of how things came to be. Sharing these stories can inspire further discoveries about the natural world.

Other Ideas
For Learning about the Earth's Forces

1. Become as adept at fire building as the early settlers of your area were. Use a fire drill or flint and steel to start a fire. See "Resources" in this chapter for help.

2. Discover the fun of making a campfire with your family. Teach the skill of building a fire and enjoy watching the flames.

3. Pin towels on kids and let their capes signal the direction and power of the wind.

4. Stay with a fire through the night. Offer it branches for fuel. Watch its flame. Feel its spirit. Reflect on the contradiction as it warms your body while it consumes part of your planet.

5. Walk outside in a rain or snow storm. Enjoy the power of nature.

6. Examine a dead animal or a decaying log. Look for signs of plants and animals that use the dead matter to survive. Talk about the cycle of life and death and the web of life.

7. Listen for the sights and sounds of mating—the drumming of grouse, the hooting of the great horned owl, spring peepers, the changes in bird calls, the rub marks of deer and moose.

8. If your compass skills are good, walk or paddle into a thick blanket of fog. Using compass bearings, try to find your way to a specific place.

9. Photograph lightning. From a safe distance, of course.

10. Climb a tree on a very windy day. Sway with the tree. But don't get blown away.

11. Cook a meal on a reflective stove, from sunlight alone.

12. Gather friends or family at the base of a waterfall. Feel its power.

Resources

Wilderness Days by Sigurd Olson. New York: Alfred A. Knopf, 1972.

"To Build A Fire," in *The Best Short Stories of Jack London.* New York: Fawcett Premier, 1962.

Making Sure-fire Tinder (Flint and Steel) by David S. Ripplinger. Osseo, MN: Track of the Wolf, Inc., 1984.

Creative Campfires (Songs and Stories) by Douglas R. Bowen. Nampa, ID: Thorne Printing Co., 1974.

Tom Brown's Field Guide to Wilderness Survival by Tom Brown. New York: Berkley Books, 1983.

Joy of Nature: How to Observe and Appreciate the Great Outdoors by Reader's Digest Association. New York: Reader's Digest Pub., 1977.

A Book of Indian Tales by Charles Wood. New York: The Vanguard Press, 1929.

American Indian Myths and Legends edited by Richard Erdoes and Alfonso Ortiz. New York: Pantheon Books, 1984.

Gift of the Sacred Dog by Paul Goble. New York: Bradbury Press, 1982.

Her Seven Brothers by Paul Goble. New York: Bradbury Press, 1988.

Discovery
is a
moment
of
awareness.

10. Solo

Time for yourself is important. Profound discoveries can be made when you are alone; free of distractions, external demands and pressures; free of the need to communicate. When you are alone with the quiet of the natural world, your vision is clearest.

The ability to be alone comfortably must be consciously developed by beginning with short, well-planned, safe solos. Skills for soloing can grow to a point where being alone is as comfortable and enjoyable as being in the company of good friends. Then you can gradually extend the length of time on these excursions.

This activity could be for adults or children. However, we have written it for children with hopes that an adult encouraging a child to solo might also be inspired.

Solo: The Story

"I have the feeling that someone is following me. Or that a bear will jump out of the woods," Ramona confided.

"It is a bit scary, but you don't have to worry. Bears will be frightened of you," Paul said, trying to reassure himself as much as his 11-year-old daughter.

Two days earlier Ramona had been in the company of her friends. Seven girls had joked and laughed, played board games, watched videos and snacked for hours. Now Paul wondered, "How will Ramona get along all by herself in the woods?"

Ramona had chosen the area for her solo: a Norway pine forest between a rocky creek and the ridge that forms the lookout for Hawk Ridge in Duluth, Minnesota. She had been in that area on several previous occasions and was familiar with the trails.

Nonetheless, Paul was concerned. He knew there was a significant difference between being in a remote area with friends and choosing to be alone in the same area.

A chilly October wind blew out of the northwest. The 50-foot pines were swaying. Together Paul and Ramona hiked into the forest. "Where should I go?" Ramona asked.

"You may want to pick an area out of the wind," Paul suggested.

"Well, this looks like a good spot. Not too wet, somewhat protected from the wind," Ramona said, settling into a cove formed by windfall and brush.

"I'll be back in one hour, at 2:15," Paul said. Meanwhile I'll hike to the ridge. You must stay in this immediate vicinity," he added, indicating an area approximately 50 yards in diameter.

Paul left and hiked the trail towards the ridge. He looked back and saw his red-haired daughter walking around her area. Then he looked down at the trail. Animal tracks were clearly imprinted in the wet soil. Deer? Dog? Wolf? He wasn't sure. "Perhaps I should stay within earshot," he thought. "Keep an eye on her just in case something happens."

A three-toed woodpecker drew his attention as it furiously scattered bark. Paul continued up the ridge, checking his watch as he climbed. It was 1:45.

Ramona, back in her solo environment, could not hear the woodpecker. She heard only the wind in the pines, which to her sounded like rushing water. She could even feel the swaying of the trees when she leaned against one for a backrest. Ramona's mind was busy. Her initial fears had vanished soon after Paul disappeared down the trail. Now she thought mostly about how to keep warm and dry.

First, she emerged from her cove to search for other dry areas. She picked up sticks and poked the soft carpet of pine needles to see if there was dry soil underneath. There was none to be found. Her cove was probably the driest spot. She broke the sticks into pieces.

"It would really be great if I could see an animal," she thought.

She scanned the forest, wondering what animals might be present—mice, rabbits, birds, deer, bear, wolves, moose. She didn't see a thing.

She returned to her cove. Now warmed from moving about, she sat still and considered her situation. "I wonder what I would do if Dad didn't come back. I could wait longer, and if he didn't return I could hike to the car. I'm sure I could find it."

Her thoughts were interrupted by a chickadee that flew into the brush near the opening to her cove. Ramona was still. The little bird flew to a branch within her reach. She was amazed. She wanted to touch it, as a greeting. Instead, she remained motionless so as not to frighten the bird. A gust of wind crashed through the woods. The moment was broken. Off flew the bird.

Ramona heard a new sound above the wind—snapping sticks, whistling. Her heart raced. Her worst fear—another person. Would he respect her right to explore the woods alone?

To her surprise and relief the sound was from Paul, walking through the pines, making a fair amount of noise. He disturbed the peace and quiet of her spot.

She met his hug, enthusiasm and inquiring glances. "It didn't seem like a very long time."

As they walked along the path, they joined hands. "Dad, did you ever do anything like this when you were a kid?" Paul searched his memory.

"Yes . . . but you know, Ramona, I'd really like to do more."

Activity

Purpose   To help children discover the value of being alone by letting them take a solo trip.

Age/Number/Setting   This works best for children 10 and older. A place away from people is essential; however, the child should be familiar with the setting.

How-To   How do you get your children to go out alone? The answer varies. The key, however, lies in the interests and the ages of the children. What do they like to do? Watch birds? Look for rocks? Collect leaves? Pick berries? Solo outings for young children should focus on one or two strong interests. Emphasize the idea of fun rather that the idea of a "solo."

However, it is important never to deceive children about a solo. They must know when, where and for how long they will be left alone. Success of the solo depends on, and builds, trust.

Select a site. The choice of site is critical. It must be safe. The child should be allowed to help select the area. Children will select a site where they feel comfortable. Older children are more trustworthy and skilled and may be able to take their solos in more rugged areas.

Plan the solo together. Choose a date and time. How long should the solo be? Some young children may be able to be alone for a maximum of 30 minutes. Others can be alone for an hour. The basic rule of thumb is that the solo must be a positive experience. Discuss details like appropriate clothing, the need for snacks, writing materials and other items.

Plan your own time. Give thought to what you are going to do during the child's solo. Explain your plans so the child will know what you will be doing and where you will be. Share your preparations and reflections with your child.

Immediately before the solo, explore the area. Describe the physical limits, discuss the area (including trails), how long you will be gone and where to meet.

Leave. Go far enough away so there is no temptation for the child to try to find you.

Immediately after the solo, spend time discussing the experience. Acknowledge the child's discoveries and your own. Often this is a time of close sharing. Savor it!

Did You Know?
Being Alone Is Important

What is a solo? A solo is an outing by oneself. It provides the opportunity for solitude and reflection. What you do on a solo is as limitless as the number of places you may go.

More than a hundred years ago, Henry David Thoreau spent two years alone at Walden Pond in Massachusetts. He supported himself from a small garden. He built a cabin and recorded his thoughts and activities in a journal. Thoreau saw his pursuit of solitude as a chance "to live deliberately, to front only the essential facts of life." What Thoreau discovered at Walden was the importance of solitude to self-understanding and to finding his place in society.

The ancient arts of yoga and meditation and the vision quest of Native Americans offer alternative pathways of solitary discovery. The Woodland Indian people felt they had a responsibility to the earth that gave them life. To find out what their particular responsibility was, they sought a private dream or vision through fasting, solitude and meditation.

Crow Dog, a Sioux spiritual leader, has described the vision quest as an opportunity "to see with the eye in one's heart, rather than the eyes in one's head."

For Sioux youth the vision quest means four days of total fasting

The vision quest is an opportunity "to see with the eye in one's heart. . . ."

Crow Dog

The
awakening
of a
deep inner life
through
an intimate
encounter with
nature.

in the wilderness. They wait for a vision, a guardian spirit, to come to them. This vision determines their future role with their people and the earth.

The process of that rite of passage has been adapted by Wilderness Vision Quest, a Virginia-based organization whose goal is to extend the knowledge and feelings of native people to others. Vision Quest offers a week-long backpacking experience designed to accomplish "the awakening of a deep, inner life through an intimate encounter with nature."

In a vision quest, the instructions are "to slow down, to be open and to listen." Participants carry with them only a backpack, a sleeping bag, canteen, small tent and personal gear.

They carry no cooking equipment because the meals they plan are simple and uncooked. Each person receives one-half pound of food per day, consisting of nuts, dried fruits and cheese.

Participants are encouraged to record thoughts in their journals in words and pictures. Another tool to help them gain a more intimate relationship with the natural world is "fascinations," a process for recording in their journals all the things that catch their attention during the day. They hike no more than three hours per day. This encourages taking time to enjoy the environment around them.

The importance of the solo experience is also reflected in the philosophies of Outward Bound, a worldwide outdoor adventure program designed to create personal growth experiences. Founder Kurt Hahn viewed the solo as "a fresh youthful experience which makes it possible once again to feel wonder and astonishment and so, contemplating, to look forward, outward and upward to new horizons."

Participants spend three days on solo. They take a sleeping bag, a tarp and a water bottle. They take no food. Individuals participating in this experience are instructed to keep a journal and document their thoughts.

In *Reflections from the North Country*, Sigurd Olson recalled many of his moments of solitude: exploring, climbing, canoeing or reading late at night. For him, solitude was the time to "iron out the wrinkles of [his] soul." Whatever the format, time or place of solo experiences, solitude is important, indeed crucial, to fostering a sense of wonder.

Other Ideas For Taking Solo Outings

1. Take a walk with a preschooler. Go outside in your back yard or neighborhood park. Respect the preschooler's need to be alone. Let him or her discover things while you only watch.

2. Take time alone outdoors during your lunch break. Record thoughts to such open-ended questions as: What do you feel, hear, smell, taste or see?

3. Plan a two- or three-day solo as a weekend backpacking, canoeing or winter camping trip. Spend time beforehand thinking about what books or writing or drawing materials to take.

4. Do a variation solo. For example, take a solo at the same spot during each season. Or take a solo at different times of the night and day in the same spot.

5. On a family outing, send everyone off in different directions for a 15-minute solo. Come together and share observations and reflections.

6. Take a small tent along on a camping trip and encourage people to spend time alone in the tent whenever they choose.

7. Take time in the early morning or at the close of the day for a daily meditation. Read a passage from an outdoor philosopher.

8. Take a silent walk—no talking or singing. Listen to the sounds of the natural world. Watch for movement. Walk as quietly as you can, slowly, with feet just gently touching the earth.

9. Use the quiet and darkness of the night to focus your thoughts. Walk a familiar trail. Paddle on a moonlit lake.

10. Challenge yourself outdoors by entering a triathalon, white-water canoe or kayaking event, orienteering contest or wilderness cross-country ski race. A commitment to train for these events takes you outdoors on a regular basis. You can experience the natural world fully in all its moods and discover more about your own inner strengths.

Resources

Reflections from the North Country by Sigurd Olson. New York: Alfred A. Knopf, 1982.

Walden by Henry David Thoreau. New York: Bantam Books, 1962.

How Nature Works: Regenerating Kinship with Planet Earth by Michael J. Cohen. Walpole:Stillpoint Publications.

America's Fascinating Indian Heritage edited by James A. Maxwell. Pleasantville, NY: Reader's Digest, 1978.

Seven Arrows by Hyemeyohsts Storm. New York: Ballantine Books, 1972.

Voices of Earth and Sky: The Vision Life of Native Americans by Vinson Brown. CA: Naturegraph Publishers, Inc., 1974.

"Wilderness Vision Quest" by Michael H. Brown, in *For the Conservation of the Earth* edited by Vince Martin. Golden, CO: Fulcrum, Inc., 1988.

"How Wilderness Facilitates Personal Growth" by John Hendee and Michael Brown. In *For the Conservation of the Earth* edited by Vince Martin. Golden, CO: Fulcrum, Inc., 1988.

365 Starry Nights: An Introduction to Astronomy for Every Night of the Year by Chet Raymo. Englewood Cliffs, NJ: Prentice-Hall, Inc., 1982.

My Side of the Mountain by Jean George. New York: Dutton, 1959.

DISCOVERY

Discovery
is a
moment
of
awareness.

11. Reflections in the Snow

February 20, 1987. "Winter solo, Boundary Waters Canoe Area, fixing supper. Is there anything so gentle as the arrival of darkness? Its gray light has crept out of the forest to embrace me. So slowly that it is imperceptible in action—much as major events in our lives. We do not recognize their significance until we are engulfed in total darkness."

Writing a journal is an opportunity to converse with yourself. As you write, your observations and thoughts become more clear. Finding the words for your journal involves a silent, internal exploration of a place you have visited, the people you have met, and the ideas you have encountered. The value of such writing is that it blends direct investigation with reflection. Your journal entries can lead you to important discoveries about yourself and the natural world.

In this story Ann recalls a solo winter camping trip and expands on the entries in the journal about that trip.

Reflections in the Snow: The Story

Ten miles of hard skiing. Breaking trail across Pipestone Bay. No visibility because of horizontal snow. Navigation by compass only.

For the past hour Ann had been planning the tasks she would need to complete when she got back to the tent. Tighten tent ropes. Move snowshoes next to the tent. Take butter and dry drink mix from the tree food bag. She would have no hot dinner.

She was exhausted, and it was snowing hard. She still had a quart of water and plenty of food left over from lunch. Once back in camp Ann quickly secured her accommodations for the night and crawled into her four-by-six-foot refuge. She took out her journal. It was 4 p.m. The sound of wind and snow attacking the tent made Ann snuggle deep into her sleeping bag. She was on her first solo trip in six years. She began to write:

"Before the snow hit at midday, I so enjoyed the tracks on the lake: wolf, moose, otter, pine marten, weasel. And all out on that large lake! I cherish the winter so much in the Boundary Waters. In all seasons it teems with life, but only in this season are the secrets of the animals really told.

"My legs are so happy to be relieved. I have that wonderful feeling of total physical exhaustion, but mental and emotional fullness. I didn't realize how much I needed time to myself. I almost didn't come, almost succumbed to the question, 'How can you go away and leave your kids and husband just to go camping for three days?' It helped to read in my book last night that in the quiet reaches of our souls the real business of life is found. It was a much needed affirmation of the importance of taking time to get in tune with myself.

"As I close my eyes, all I can visualize is a set of parallel tracks disappearing into infinity. Tracks leading to hazy, uncertain images. A struggle to get there. I must search and search for the tracks. But as in my life's path, there is reward at the end."

Slowly, almost imperceptibly, the wind diminished. Now the only sound on the tent came from huge snowflakes landing on the fabric. They sounded big, almost like raindrops. Ann was nearly oblivious to the outside world. Her immediate reality was a five-by-seven inch, spiral-bound notebook that she had purchased at the dime store for 99 cents. Buying the notebook had been a spontaneous act, as had buying the small box of colored pencils next to the notebook. She was shopping with the kids for a cousin's birthday present when she walked down the school supply aisle.

"If I'm going to do some serious writing on my trip, I should have a notebook just for the trip," she had thought.

The gesture was significant. She was making a commitment not to write letters, but simply to write for herself.

It grew dark in the tent, so Ann lit her candle lantern and continued to write, not quite ready to nap. By 7 p.m. she had written 25 pages in her notebook. Only then did she think to notice the time. She was surprised to find that she had been writing for three hours.

There were pages about her relationship with her two children, with her husband, with several close friends. She used her colored pencils to draw an intricate map of her route that day. She had commented on the inspiration her children had given her to draw—to work at letting go of the conviction that she couldn't draw. There was a long list of questions about future professional directions. There was reflection on past priorities and choices. And there was an urgent analysis of how to begin to simplify her life, to be more in touch with the earth's rhythms.

Not that I choose to hide from the world. Far from it. My problem is that I'm too immersed in it. Unbalanced in favor of the secular business of life. It's scary to think about changing balances. Overwhelming. But I want to start . . . somewhere.

It was the sound of another living creature that brought Ann back to the Boundary Waters Canoe Area. In the nearly complete silence of the winter wilderness night she heard: *"Who cooks-for-you? Who-cooks-for-you—ah?"* She smiled and began to write again.

"Beautiful. Two barred owls calling back and forth across my bay. Creatures of the night, signaling the beginning of activity. How different their life is from mine! Yet, I feel befriended, almost embraced. I am one with this place."

The winter wilderness morning arrived more quietly than the dawn of other seasons. No chorus of impatient birds, save the lone squawk of the raven. No lapping of waves on the shore of the lake, no rustle of leaves by eager squirrels. The morning was silent.

After a long, restful night Ann broke the silence by lighting her backpacking stove. Today was the long trek out. Thoughts of pulling the heavily loaded sled through new, wet snow back across four lakes and five portages had persuaded her to have a hot breakfast. As she waited for the water to boil, she began writing again in her journal. Piece by piece she considered the equipment she had brought. She was committed to repeating this trip next year and wanted to be better prepared.

The equipment analysis continued as she ate oatmeal and drank three cups of hot chocolate. She drew an image of her favorite camping cup and made her last journal entry of the trip.

Can any pleasure be more profound than the heat from a cup of hot chocolate on such a morning? I am soothed by the image of rising steam, by feeling the warmth travel down inside me. I think an overriding reason why the lure of camping is so strong for me is that I need to get back in touch with simple rhythms and needs. That connectedness gives me guidance through the maze of complexity and artificiality that is modern life.

Activity

Purpose
: To use journal entries as the medium for reflections on an outdoor experience.

Age/Number/Setting
: Age 10 and up. Anywhere.

Materials
: Something to write on and a pen or pencil.

How-To
: Select a journal. Durability, flexibility and portability are important considerations. Some people prefer the casualness of a spiral-bound notebook. Others need the specialness of a commercially produced journal.

When you are outdoors, take your journal along. Find a natural object and observe it. Think about its colors, shadows, sounds, smells, feelings. Make a sketch. Write in detail about the object or scene.

Write in your journal about things that are important. Capture and preserve the stages of growth of a child. Record memories from a family camping trip. Take note of seasonal changes. Pay closer attention to the details on outdoor adventures.

At the end of a hike or long paddle, take time to reflect. Sit down with paper, pencil and a watch in a quiet place. Write nonstop about *anything* for 10 minutes. Write about what you have done that day, and about what you are thinking. Don't worry about grammar or punctuation or form. Repeat the exercise over a period of several weeks. You have the beginnings of a journal.

Include drawings in your journal. They needn't be more than a map or little symbol or even stick people. The activity of drawing may help you when words don't come easily.

Reread your journal. It is at least as important to read your journal as it is to write in it. At one moment your writing may appear morose, in the next upbeat. Why? What prompted the change? Being able to pinpoint the reason for mood changes can lead you to a greater understanding of your own needs.

Did You Know?
Famous Discoveries Have Been Recorded in Journals

The words "diary" and "journal" both come from the Latin word for "daily." Regular or periodic writing distinguishes diary and journal keeping from other forms of autobiographical writing like memoirs and autobiographies. Diaries and journals are generally not retrospective. They are written day-by-day.

The earliest journals were community records that predated written language. For example, certain tribes of Plains Indians regularly had a gathering of the elders to decide which seasonal events should be recorded in their paintings and on their tepee walls.

More recently, journals of explorers have shed important light on historical events. The diaries of explorers like Lewis and Clark and John Wesley Powell carried valuable information about large, uncharted stretches of the West. They still make great reading today.

The journals of women provide much historical information on lifestyle issues ranging from child-rearing, to foods, to homes and relationships. Elizabeth Cady Stanton, Agatha Christie, Abigail

Elders decided which events should be recorded on tepee walls.

Adams, Anne Morrow Lindbergh and Anais Nin are of just a few well-known women whose published diaries offer important insights into their times as well as into their personal lives.

Journals are far more than a simple recounting of facts. They provide historical perspectives and visions of new places, as well as personal insights. Often they read like first-class literature. They can be inspirational to their readers and their writers.

Other Ideas
For Writing about Outdoor Experiences

1. Help a child start a journal. It can be a scrapbook of cards, awards, letters or artwork related to outdoor activities.

2. Keep a sketch journal of a trip, either a map of where you've been or pictures of things you've seen.

3. Record an audio journal with a small tape recorder. Capture sounds from a natural setting; add your comments.

4. Create a photo journal by dating and writing notes alongside the pictures of outings. Include photos of people, places and events.

5. At the end of an outdoor adventure, gather everyone together in a circle. Compose a group journal of shared thoughts by passing a "talking stone" around the circle. The person holding the stone shares remembrances and insights.

6. Give a child a notebook and a pencil. Have her choose a spot that is only a few minutes away. Explain that she is to walk there, sit down and remain there for 15 to 30 minutes. During that time she should record the sights and sounds she notices.

7. Make a collage out of magazine pictures or natural materials to show discoveries of the day. Work alone or in a group.

8. Create a map of a trip. Show where you traveled. Make a timeline. Describe what you did along the way.

Resources

Keeping Your Personal Journal by George F. Simons. New York: Ballantine Books, 1978.

Writing for Kids by Carol Lea Benjamin. New York: T.Y. Crowell, 1985.

Diary of an Edwardian Lady by Edith Holden. London, England: Webb and Bower, 1977.

Janet Marsh's Nature Diary by Janet Marsh. London: Michael Joseph, 1979.

The Naturalist's Sketchbook: Pages from the Seasons of a Year by Clare Leslie. New York: Dodd-Mead, 1987.

Drawing from Nature by Jim Arnoshy. New York: Lothrop, Lee and Shepard, 1982.

The Earth Speaks: An Acclimatization Journal edited by Steve Van Matre and Bill Weiler. Warrenville, IL: The Institute for Earth Education, 1983.

Listen to Nature by Joseph Cornell. Nevada City, CA: Dawn Publications, 1987.

Women and Wilderness by Anne LaBastille. San Francisco: Sierra Club Books, 1980.

Walking Softly in the Wilderness: The Sierra Club Guide to Backpacking by John Hart. San Francisco: Sierra Club Books, 1984.

Sharing is the affirmation of discovery. By sharing a discovery about the natural world with another person, the experience is enhanced.

The process of sharing facts and feelings connected with major, meaningful discoveries creates a bridge between individuals, cultures and generations. Through sharing the history of the culture is passed on, and a connection between the past and the future is established.

Sharing can be accomplished in many different ways. Everyone has favorite personal styles for sharing themselves and the deep, touching experiences that they treasure. The activities in this section are designed to encourage people to share through whatever creative form of expression best fits the situation and their own needs.

So share a discovery through creative expression—a story, a song, a poem or a picture. Creativity captures and communicates the soul of a discovery.

Or share a discovery by taking someone along on the experience. Go for a walk with a friend or family member to a special beach. Or go backpacking or paddling on a favorite stretch of river. Shared outings are essential for introducing family and friends to the sense of wonder.

Or share by teaching others. A teacher points out the signs of a moose bed and shares his excitement about discovering the matted grass, hair or rub marks. Teaching with a sense of wonder is more than imparting knowledge. It is revealing an attitude toward the discovery.

Powerful feelings compel people to share. But sharing can often be difficult because it is risky. By sharing what is closest to your heart, you make yourself vulnerable and you risk not being understood. Yet it is in sharing that we grow in self-confidence and self-discovery.

Sharing is a skill that can be learned. So practice. Take others outside. Share stories, drawings or songs from a trip. Design experiences that encourage the sharing of perceptions, memories, and the discoveries that you've made about your world.

SHARING

12. Chuck the Penguin

Storytelling is universal. Myths and legends exist in all cultures. From ancient Ojibwe tales to 20th century bedtime stories, the oral tradition continues. It continues because of the bond it creates between parent and child, elders and young people.

Stories also can come from your own experiences. Often the most lively and meaningful stories are extensions of your life. Stories transfer significant events, dreams, discoveries and people into lasting memories.

In the following story a father transforms his love for the mysterious continent of Antarctica into a lively, informative story about the explorers and wildlife of the earth's coldest continent.

Chuck the Penguin: The Story

"All right, kids. Storytime's over," said Grant. "Now hop into bed."

Ben and Carolyn raced up the stairs to see who would be the first in bed. Grant picked up the storybooks and followed. He leaned over to kiss Carolyn goodnight, but she was hiding under the covers, near the bottom of the bed.

"Where's Carolyn?" he played along.

"She's right there," said Ben.

"Ben!" screamed Carolyn indignantly.

"Come on, you two. The sun went down an hour ago," Grant coaxed. "It's your bedtime."

"Dad, could we have just one more story?" pleaded Ben. "How about Chuck the Penguin?"

Grant's resistance was low. Chuck the Penguin stories evolved from his favorite topic—Antarctic exploration. He had been making up these stories for over a year. Grant was fascinated by the cold, white, farthest reaches of the earth. He liked to translate his own dream of an Antarctic expedition into imaginary characters.

Grant sat down on Ben's bed, leaning back against the wall. "Chuck was an Emperor Penguin," he began.

"What's an em-per?" interrupted Carolyn.

"A king," answered Grant. "The Emperor Penguin has bright orange feathers on its head. It looks like a crown."

"Are there princess penguins, too?" asked four-year-old Carolyn.

Grant smiled. "No, but there are King and Royal Penguins."

"Come on, Dad. Tell us what happens to Chuck," Ben said impatiently.

"Chuck lived in a colony with hundreds of other Emperor Penguins. That means they lived together in the same place, like the herd of buffalo you saw last summer on the prairie."

"How big were they?" asked Ben.

"Well, about as tall as Carolyn," Grant said. Carolyn raised her three-foot stature in bed. "And they weighed more than you, Ben: 55 to 100 pounds."

"Wow!" said Ben and Carolyn.

"What made them so heavy?" asked Ben.

"They are heavy to help them swim under the water," said Grant. "Unlike flying birds, their bones are solid. They also have an inch of fat, or blubber, around their bodies to keep them warm during the Antarctic winter."

"How cold does it get?" asked Ben, snuggling deeper under his blankets.

"Well, remember this morning when it got to 30 below and you could hear the trees crack?" asked Grant.

"And we had a frozen water pump," Carolyn chimed in.

"Yes. Well, imagine a place twice that cold, with no light or warmth from the sun," continued Grant.

"And that's where Chuck lives?" asked Carolyn.

"At the very bottom of the world," Ben responded.

SHARING: Chuck the Penguin

"Chuck the Penguin lived on Ross Island just off the Antarctic Coast," said Grant. "It was a wonderful place to live, with lots of things to eat —crabs, squid, fish and krill (a small, shrimplike animal)."

"Yech!" both kids exclaimed, tongues sticking out.

"Well, Chuck liked it," Grant said. "It was cold down there, and nothing much could hurt him."

"Was there anything bad there?"

"Well, things in the water like killer whales and leopard seals could eat them, but the penguins watched carefully," assured Grant.

"One day, Chuck was out swimming when he saw a ship come near the island. The ship had two big words on its side—Terra Nova. It meant New Land and was the name of the ship. The ship was owned by the British Navy. The man in charge was Robert Falcon Scott.

"Chuck watched the ship as it sailed up and down the coast trying to find a good place to drop anchor. Captain Scott wanted to camp near the colony of penguins but the ice was rotten and the rock cliffs too steep. So the ship went to Cape Evans over 100 miles away. Chuck was curious; he followed the ship."

"Is this real, Dad?" asked Ben. His six-year-old mind was keen on finding out what was real and what was a story.

"Oh, yes, Scott really did go to Antarctica. He wanted to be the first to get to the South Pole. But he also wanted to find out what lived down there. One of the things he planned to collect was penguin eggs," said Grant.

"The expedition to get the penguin eggs took the scientists five weeks. It was a very hard journey—blizzards, temperatures ranging from minus 15 to minus 75, even during the day, and little daylight. Some days they only traveled one or two miles. They had a hundred miles to go. They crossed barrier ice and went over deep crevasses."

"How come they did it, then?" asked Ben. "Couldn't they just stay inside the hut all winter and play?"

"Well, they wanted to know more about the penguin eggs. Scientists are interested in how things work, how things live—just as you are."

"Did Chuck tell the mama penguins to hide their eggs?" asked Ben.

"He warned the daddy penguins because the mama penguins were out feeding at sea during the winter. Once the mama lays the egg, she needs to eat. So the daddy penguin sits on the egg for two months, keeping it warm under a special flap of skin under his belly."

"Were the eggs white?" asked Ben.

"Yes."

"If they were white maybe the scientists couldn't find them on top of the ice," said Ben.

"That's a good idea," said Grant.

"I hope the scientists didn't take all the eggs," said Ben.

The scientists only wanted a few," Grant said, "and they didn't hurt the penguins."

"Did the scientists get Chuck the Penguin's egg?" asked Carolyn.

"No, he knew they were coming, so he camped on the other side of the colony. Remember, there were hundreds of penguins. The explorers never got to Chuck's spot," Grant reassured his kids.

"How big were the eggs?" asked Carolyn.

"Six to seven inches," said Grant.

"Did the penguins get them back?" asked Ben hopefully.

"No. But the next year the penguins had another egg," Grant replied.

"How did you learn about penguins?" asked Ben. "Did you ever go the Antarctica?"

"No, but I'd like to someday," said Grant as he tucked the kids in their beds. "Until then, I'll keep reading about them and dreaming. And that's what I want you to do! Good night. See you in the morning."

Activity

Purpose
To create and share a nature story.

Age/Number/Setting
Five-year-olds to eighty-five-year-olds (and beyond!) can make up their own tales. Settings vary from bedtime to campfires, from car traveling to hiking, from mealtimes to rest times by a lake or creek.

Materials
Natural objects for inspiration or for props. Reference books or storybooks on the topic.

How-To
The best stories are built upon experiences in your own life. "My biggest . . . ," "My favorite . . . ," "What happened the day I. . . ."

Add fantasy or fascinating facts to your tale by reading about the places, objects or creatures involved in your experience. For "Chuck the Penguin," Grant read the journals of polar explorers and children's books on the natural history of penguins.

Characters. Limit the story to one or two main characters. That makes it easier to follow the plot. Describe what the animal or plant looks like. Then let the children name it. It is preferable to have the main character be the same age or have some of the same qualities as the listener.

Imagination
abounds
within us all.
It awaits only
an audience.

Place. With your children, describe the land the character lives on—colors, geographical and physical surroundings. Help listeners compare the story setting to the place where they live, noting both similarities and differences.

Plot. Each story should have a beginning, middle and end. Often in making up a story, you will have only a beginning in mind. With luck and imagination, the main character and your audience will help out. Let them create the action!

Storytelling. The best storytellers get totally involved in the tale—body, mind and spirit. Raising and lowering the voice, pausing, eye contact and hand gestures help create the story.

Questions. Don't be afraid of questions. It's all part of sharing. And if you don't know an answer, look it up together.

Encourage children and other listeners to try storytelling. Imagination abounds within us all. It awaits only an audience.

Did You Know?
Stories Share Many Lessons

The path to physical exploration of the natural world is paved with books. Books that tell how to identify a bird, insect, plant or animal track. Books that tell how to canoe, build a fire, camp or fish. Books that inspire or teach through a story.

A child is a tough critic. She has little time for slow introductions, weakly developed characters or "preachy" endings. She may listen to a story once, but will not ask for it again unless it has adventure, intriguing characters, believability and inspiration.

Stories must have
adventure,
intriguing characters,
believability
and
inspiration.

Early in the century, children's nature story books were typically stories of individual animals endowed with humanlike characteristics. Ernest Thompson Seton made this style famous in *Wild Animals I Have Known*.

Another great classic in this style is *The Wind in the Willows* by Kenneth Grahame. This story records the adventures of Grahame's spirited characters—Toad and Mole, Badger and Rat.

Thorton Burgess wrote a series of bedtime stories entitled *Mother West Wind Stories* for his creatures in Green Meadow. A more recent author who uses her intimate knowledge of animals' ways to weave a strong animal main character is Jean Craighead George. In *Julie of the Wolves* she portrays a beautiful relationship that develops between a lost Eskimo girl and a wolf pack. *Dipper of Copper Creek* and *Vulpes the Fox* are two examples of her strong stories of natural history.

In *Charlotte's Web* E.B. White helps readers sense the trials and joys of a spider, Charlotte, her barnyard friends and a little girl who took the time to watch and listen.

Other natural history writers portray relationships between children and pets. In *Rascal,* Sterling North enables the reader to see the world through the eyes of a raccoon and a boy who learns to think like a raccoon. *Where the Red Fern Grows* by Wilson Rawls vividly portrays the relationship between a boy, his two coon dogs and the Ozark mountains.

During the past 20 years, authors have begun to write about pressing environmental problems. In 1971, noted children's author Theodore Geissel, better known as Dr. Seuss, paved the way with *The Lorax*. This book shows its respect for a child's ability to understand ecological principles by describing the terrible "antics of the Onceler." Seuss's most recent environmentally conscious story, *The Butter Battle Book*, employs his unique scheme of rhyming words and imaginary characters in a chilling look at the realities of the cold war and the potential for world nuclear war.

Author Carol Carrick and her illustrator husband Donald Carrick show a sensitivity for the natural world in their outdoor adventure books. *A Clearing in the Forest* and *Lost in the Storm* both depict people in harsh environments who come to new understandings because of their acceptance of the ways of nature. In a somewhat different style, the husband and wife team created *The Brook,* which is a beautiful mood piece about the arrival of spring.

Robert McCloskey also writes gentle nature stories. In *Time of Wonder,* this winner of the coveted Caldecott Award shows the joys and adventures of spending a summer vacation on an island of Maine's Penobscot Bay. McCloskey's *Blueberries for Sal* is a delightful story about the blueberry-picking adventures of two moms and two youngsters on Blueberry Hill. There are some striking similarities between Sal's mom and the brown, furry mom.

Byrd Baylor's poetic prose about the life of creatures in the desert southwest comes alive with the powerful illustrations of Peter Parnall. *Hawk, I Am Your Brother* and *Amigo* both speak to the connectedness between wild animals and children who take the time to understand them. The books teach and inspire a powerful respect for wild creatures. Baylor and Parnall's most recent book, *I'm in Charge of Celebrations,* captures the essence of keeping a sense of wonder—time outdoors with senses *alert.*

The natural and cultural history of the land is another style in children's earth stories. The Laura Ingalls Wilder books, like *Little House in the Big Woods, On the Banks of Plum Creek* and *Little House on the Prairie* are a rich tapestry of homespun lore for readers of all ages. The love of days gone by is captured in a simple, lively narrative about a girl and her family as they stake claims in various parts of pioneer America.

The essence of keeping a sense of wonder— time outdoors with senses alert.

Most nature stories for children can be placed in one of the above-mentioned six categories: animals with human-like characteristics, pet/child relationships, a child's view of pressing environmental problems, outdoor adventure books, sensory awareness, and cultural or natural histories. Essential elements necessary in all forms are the accuracy of the environmental information and the importance of our relationship with the earth. Both are critical in creating a good earth story.

Other Ideas
For Creative Sharing

1. *Creation Stories.* Most cultures have stories about the beginning of the world and why certain things in nature are the way they are. Learn a Native American creation story and tell it to someone. Sources include: *Keepers of the Earth* by Michael Caduto, *Tales the Elders Told* by Basil H. Johnston and *Legends* by Adolf Hungry Wolf. In learning a tale, read it over and over. Details and repetitions within the story are important. Try telling it out loud to yourself with a mirror, then tell the story to someone else.

2. *Runes.* A rune is a tale of magic and mystery. Go outside and walk around. Pick out an interesting object—an agate, a pine tree, a tadpole, a star. Look at it carefully. Imagine how it came to be. Take a friend to that spot and tell them the story.

3. *Flannel Board.* Telling a story with flannel material (or chalk and a chalk board, or construction paper) is a good way of creating a group story after a hike. Have different colors of flannel, glue and scissors set out ahead of time. Talk about what you saw together, then have everyone create one piece for the story. After everyone is finished cutting, have someone begin the story by placing a cutout on a felt-lined picture board and telling the group something about it. Keep going until everyone has had a turn.

4. *Sense of Wonder Circle.* Think about the things you saw during a hike—fields, mountains, sun, stars, moon, people, animals, plants. Then, using scissors, felt, construction paper or old

magazines, cut pictures or symbols for each of the things remembered. Arrange them in a circle. Have people create a line of poetry or prose to go with the pictures.

5. *Group Poem.* After an outdoor adventure, have the entire group create a poem. Pass around a sheet of paper and have everyone add a phrase. Read the lines to young children and ask them what they want you to write. Once complete read the poem to the group.

6. *Group Story.* One person begins a story and then drops it at any point. The next person continues. People who are timid may contribute only a little but can still be a part of the group story.

7. *Earth Music.* Be adventuresome with earth music. Compose your own song by picking a familiar tune and writing your own verses. Take a tape recorder outside to make a collection of sounds. Make natural instruments—a blade of grass or willow whistles, rhythm instruments from dried gourds, drums from hollow logs.

8. *Drama.* Plays and puppet shows provide opportunities for sharing information about the natural world. Guidelines for creating a play are similar to that of storytelling—focus on one concept, like a historical story or an incident of caring for the earth.

9. *Charades.* Use the art of pantomime to teach a natural history lesson. Charades can be done with people of any age, indoors or out. Pantomime a favorite plant or animal or a living creature that is in danger of becoming extinct. Or limit the category to an animal with a good sense of smell, animals and plants of a particular area, or a person whose job is helpful to the environment.

Resources

Choosing Books for Kids: Choosing the Right Book for the Right Child at the Right Time by Joanne Oppenheim, Barbara Brenner and Betty Boegehold. New York: Ballantine Books, 1986.

The New Read-Aloud Handbook by Jim Treleuse. New York: Penguin Books, 1989.

Creative Storytelling: Choosing, Inventing and Sharing Tales for Children by Jack Maguire. New York: McGraw-Hill Book Co., 1985.

The Call of Stories: Teaching and Moral Imagination by Robert Cole. Boston: Houghton Mifflin, 1989.

Keepers of the Earth by Michael Caduto and Joseph Bruchac. Golden, CO: Fulcrum, Inc., 1988.

Teacher's Guide to Keepers of the Earth by Michael Caduto and Joseph Bruchac. Golden, CO: Fulcrum, Inc., 1988.

Beginnings: Creation Myths of the World by Penelope Farmer. New York: Atheneum, 1979.

The Earth Song Book by Douglas Wood. St. Paul, MN: Science Museum of Minnesota, 1985.

Jumping, Laughing, and Resting: Songs for Children 3 to 10 by Evelyn Challis. New York: Amsco Publications, 1984.

Rise Up Singing: 1200 Songs, Words, Chords and Sources. Bethlehem, PA: Sing-Out Publications, 1988.

Talking to the Sun: An Illustrated Anthology of Poems for Young People selected by Kenneth Koch and Kate Farrell. New York: The Metropolitan Museum of Art/Henry Holt and Co., 1985.

13. On the Ropes

A wealth of expertise awaits those who want to learn more about the outdoors. Nature centers, environmental learning centers, summer camps, ranger naturalist programs and Audubon field trips are all great ways to learn. Likewise, universities offer lecture series, science museums lead field courses, and community education centers sponsor outings. These programs provide unparalleled opportunities for family growth through shared outdoor adventures.

These activities emphasize the quality of family sharing that is inspired by learning skills outdoors. In this story a family shares a winter weekend at a residential learning center. Working together, and yet also alone as individuals, they overcome challenging physical obstacles to build a new sense of family unity.

On the Ropes: The Story

Ramona looked up at her mother who was inching her way slowly along a narrow beam 25 feet above the earth.

Ramona could see that her mom was scared, and she was scared too. But this was the year that Mary and Ramona both had planned to complete the Adventure Ropes course at the Environmental Learning Center in northern Minnesota.

Each of the past two years Ramona had gotten as far as the beam, had become frightened and then had climbed back down. As Ramona watched her mother successfully walk to the end of the beam, she confided in the naturalist who was helping her, "This year I'm going to make it."

As her mom neared the end of the course, 12-year-old Ramona got ready to begin. The safety line was snapped into her harness, and the naturalist belayed Ramona up the first incline. With the reassuring directions of the naturalist from the ground, Ramona carefully reattached the safety line at each rung of the ladder. She adjusted her blue ear muffs, then paused and looked to the end of the course. She saw Mary on the final platform.

Ramona directed her attention to the beam. The wind pierced her jacket and sent a chill deep within. Three steps onto the beam, her goosebumps turned to tremors. Her legs, normally strong and disciplined from years of ballet, wobbled like those of a young filly.

"I-I-I-I don't h-have any c-c-c-control," she finally blurted out.

"Just keep moving. Slowly keep walking. You're doing super!" coached the naturalist from below.

Ramona finally got across the beam and reached the "hugging tree." The tree at the end of the beam held a platform so narrow that the climbers had to hug the tree for support. She held tight and peered from behind the hugging tree. She could see that her mother was now on the ground and was being embraced by friends and her dad. She could see her smiling.

Ramona started forward again. She easily negotiated the swinging bridge, but froze at the start of the Postman's Walk, a 50-foot gap spanned only by two steel cables.

"You can do it, Ramona. You look great. Just great. All right, that's it, yeah!" said Mary, now safely on the ground. She offered moral support as Ramona edged out. Ramona was too short to grab the upper cable, so she held onto the safety line the spotter had attached to the cable.

So tight was her grip on the cable that her feet touched the wire only lightly. So lightly that a gust of wind blew her feet off to the side. She was swinging from the sky hook. It held her securely. She pulled her feet back onto the walking cable.

Her brother Galen joined the others with encouraging words. "Hey, Ramona, you're gonna make it!" he shouted.

At last she reached the final wooden platform. Her thoughts went to her sixth-grade teacher. Just one day earlier she had shared with Mr. Pachioti that she was accompanying her family to the Learning Center.

"Are you going to do the Adventure Ropes course?" he had asked. When Ramona responded in the affirmative, he had shared his fear of the final jump, a free fall along a 20-foot cable aided only by a pulley strap. He also shared his joy at completing it.

"I've got to finish this," Ramona thought. "Mr. Pachioti will ask if I completed the course." She closed her eyes, counted to five and leaped.

Down . . . down . . . down she slid. She opened her eyes and saw hands reaching out to slow her. To welcome her.

"I did it!" she exclaimed.

Mary, Paul, and Galen hugged her. Warmth met the cold. Ice melted and flowed down their ruddy faces like a spring thaw.

Activity

Purpose To share an outdoor adventure with your family by participating in a formally-organized outdoor program.

Age/Number/Setting Look for programs that specialize in families. They include programming for the preschooler in your family as well as the teenager and the grandparent. These programs are available all across the country in all kinds of terrain.

Materials Participation in formal programs often requires a fee.

How-To Find out about outdoor and environmental education programs offered in your area. See "Other Ideas" for suggestions on where to look for such program listings. Are the programs within your budget? Do they offer activities geared to your interests, skill levels and needs? Are activities individual or family oriented?

Ask about a particular program. Are the accommodations and equipment in good repair? What are the qualifications of the staff? Is the food good? How much class time is spent indoors versus outdoors? How large are classes? Is there enough equipment for each class member?

Sign up! Build family interest with periodic discussion of plans. Study a map to learn about the area where the program is located. Discuss the kinds of activities that will be offered. Encourage everyone to think about the activities that most intrigue them.

Involve everyone in the packing and preparation. Preschoolers should take some personal belongings in a small pack—a favorite stuffed animal, books, or toys. In a new place, on a new adventure, it is helpful for every family member to take along something familiar and comforting.

Ultimately, of course, parents must assume responsibility for what is packed. But the more that a sense of teamwork is established from the beginning, the greater the chance that the program will serve as a unifying function for your family.

Encourage each family member to participate in activities. Younger, timid ones may need adult companionship. Share the care of infants so that both parents have an opportunity for new adventure.

Find a daily time in the program when the family can gather. It might be mealtime or bedtime. All family members should gather and share highlights from the day.

Continue to share the experience after it is over. Stories at mealtimes, family slide shows, or letter writing and phone calls are all important ways to let the program continue to be a growing experience for family members.

Did You Know?
Our Children Inspired Us
To Teach

Our Sense of Wonder teaching began with an invitation from Jack Pichotta, Director of the Wolf Ridge Environmental Learning Center in northern Minnesota. "We have great natural history classes and superb teachers," he commented. "The combination of the two instills a sense of curiosity and a respect for living things in most kids. But it seems that should happen by design, not just by chance."

We talked with him about our personal joy of being outdoors and how we might share that feeling with the thousands of school-age children who come to environmental learning centers.

Wolf Ridge Environmental Learning Center offers programs typical of those available at residential centers throughout the United States. At Wolf Ridge, canoes and lakes, skis and miles of trails, climbing walls, a ropes course and a wealth of natural resource laboratory equipment are complemented by a staff that is committed to helping people learn through experience in the outdoors. The teachers infuse their programs with their own enthusiasm for nature, whatever the climate or terrain.

Since we love to share the outdoors with our own children, we accepted Jack's invitation. In 1983 we sponsored our first Sense of Wonder weekend. We searched for stream creatures, painted our faces while tracking cookie monsters, and sang songs in a sharing circle. That first weekend convinced us that family weekends could be very beneficial to all.

Currently we teach one fall weekend at Wolf Ridge and another at

Instill
a sense
of curiosity
and
a respect
for living things.

We teach
with a spirit
of play
and excitement.

Hawk Ridge Nature Preserve in Duluth, Minnesota. The second weekend is sponsored by the Duluth Audubon Society. We also teach a winter weekend at Wolf Ridge; a spring weekend among the rolling hills of the Central Wisconsin Environmental Station, and a summer week at Camp Manito-wish YMCA in the Northeast Wisconsin lakes district.

We teach with a spirit of play and excitement. But we teach differently in each place. Our key is listening to the spirit of the land.

In the major winter cold spell of 1989, we found ourselves at Wolf Ridge with 30 other parents and children at 20 below zero. Wind chills registered 60 below. We asked ourselves what survives—even grows in weather like this? Ice! We gathered small containers and filled them with water to create ice sculptures. A little bit of food coloring added the magic ingredient to the designs we created.

The new moon in August inspired us to buy a dozen glowsticks. We gathered with many families outside the nature lodge at Camp Manito-wish and set out on a firefly hike. Our glowsticks danced in the dark as we marched through the woods.

Camping outside on the eve of our Hawk Ridge family day in the fall, we sat beneath a harvest moon and were astounded at the number of sparrows and warblers migrating through the woods at night. When we woke the next morning, we changed our lesson plan and decided to migrate like the birds, using all our senses to get us "home."

Wherever we teach, we spend time getting a feeling for the spirit of the place—the quiet of a sultry summer day, the energy of a raging blizzard in winter, the burst of fall color or the smell of spring flowers pushing through the earth. The earth is our teacher; we design and interpret activities by following its lead.

Other Ideas
For Finding Family Outdoor programs

1. *Youth Organizations.* Almost every community has its Boy Scout, Girl Scout, YMCA, YWCA and 4-H organizations. Participating as a volunteer in these organizations can be rewarding in itself, providing continuing opportunities for learning new outdoor skills and for joining in camping and related educational trips. Some of these organizations also offer classes and recreational activities like weekend and week-long family camps.

2. *Camp programs.* Throughout the United States thousands of residential camps offer programs for kids as well as for families, church and civic groups. Many of these camps and their programs are accredited by the American Camping Association, Bradford Woods, 5000 SR 6710, Martinsville, IN 46151. The *Peterson's Guide, Summer Opportunities for Kids and Teenagers,* also lists hundreds of camps, schools and summer programs.

3. *Parks and recreation programs.* Most communities feature a variety of parks and recreation programs ranging from volleyball leagues and swimming lessons to photography clubs, field trips and camp programs. Contact your city, county or state parks and recreation agency to request more information.

4. *Nature centers and residential environmental education centers.* Nature centers offer a variety of seasonal programs of interest to all ages—ranging from bird watching hikes and star gazing programs to workshops and full courses on natural history topics and outdoor skills. Residential environmental centers, which usually focus on weekday programs for schools, often cater to families during weekends and summers. To find out where such centers are located, contact your school district, state department of education or natural resource agencies. Some states produce directories of their nature and environmental education centers.

5. *Universities, science museums and community schools.* These institutions offer a great variety of programs ranging from indoor lectures and movies to extended outdoor expeditions. Contact campuses to learn more about their offerings related to the environment, natural history, outdoor skills and family activities. The Natural Science for Youth Foundation, 130 Azale Drive, Roswell, GA 33075 also publishes a directory of museum nature centers.

6. *The National Audubon Society, the Sierra Club and other environmental organizations.* Both the National Audubon Society and the Sierra Club offer extensive outdoor programs, either through their local chapters or through their national offices. The National Audubon Society also operates several summer camps that specialize in nature study and environmental issues. The National Association for Environmental Education, P.O. Box 400, Troy, OH 45373, provides a full range of services, including workshops and expeditions, of interest to educators.

Resources:

Cowstails and Cobras by Karl Rohnke. Hamilton, MA: Project Adventure, 1977.

Outdoor Adventure Activities for School and Recreation Programs by Paul Darst and George Armstrong. Minneapolis: Burgess Publishing Co., 1980.

Outdoor Education: A Manual for Teaching in Nature's Classroom by Mike Link. Englewood Cliffs, N.J.: Prentice-Hall, Inc., 1981.

Sharing the Joy of Nature by Joseph Cornell. Nevada City, CA: Ansada Publications, 1989.

Humanizing Environmental Education: A Guide for Leading Nature and Human Nature Activities by Clifford Knapp and Joel Goodman. Martinville, IN: American Association, 1981.

Acclimatization: A Sensory and Conceptual Approach to Ecological Involvement by Steve Van Matre. Martinville, IN: American Camping Assoc., 1972.

The Leaders Guide to Nature-Oriented Activities by Betty Vander Smissen and Oswald Goering. Ames: Iowa State Univ. Press, 1977.

Enjoying Nature with Your Family by Michael Chinery. New York: Crown Publishers, Inc., 1977.

Hands-On Nature: Information and Activities for Exploring the Environment with Children edited by Jenepher Lingelbach. Woodstock, VT: Vermont Institute of Natural Science, 1988.

The Interpreter's Guidebook: Techniques for Programs and Presentations by Kathleen Harris Regnier, Michael Gross and Ron Zimmerman. Stevens Point, WI: University of Wisconsin Stevens Point Foundation Press, Inc., 1992.

14. The Bunkhouse

Somewhere you have a special place, a manifestation of your heart's deepest love. For a fisherman the place might be a treasured fishing hole. For a kayaker it could be a secret set of rapids. For a gardener it might be an experimental corner of the garden. For a hiker it could be a hilltop. For a family, it may be a summer cabin.

A special place beckons you to be there because you are part of it and it is a part of you. You go there seeking a friend—the comfort of familiarity. You go there to dream, to seek new visions, to reflect and to rejoice.

If you're lucky, someone will enter your life who is worthy of sharing the intimacy of your special place with you. Friend or family, you want this person to share your enthusiasm, to feel the magic that adds so much to your life. This story is about sharing. In sharing a special place, the intimacy of friendship and place take on new meaning.

The Bunkhouse: The Story

"Now we are descending into the Great River Basin," Marina's dad ceremoniously announced. Marina looked at her mom in the cab of the truck and then at her kids. They all smiled. Just a mile to go. The truck moved slowly over the rutted logging road, under tipped spruce trees and around alder thickets.

When they reached the Bunkhouse, the three-generation team worked to haul sleeping bags, lanterns and food into their family cabin. Soon the warmth of the homemade barrel stove drove off the November chill. They stood close together in front of the stove, looking out the window to the river which tumbled over the rocks 25 feet below. Their silence was a toast to being at the Bunkhouse again.

"The river is high for this time of year," Marina thought as she began to spread out sleeping bags in the loft. She could hear the river surge over the rocks, boiling with energy. She thought about the first time she, her mom and dad, brother and sisters had seen the river.

Fifteen years earlier her dad had discovered lots for lease on the Cascade River. On a foggy, rain-drenched day he gathered the family to go see them. During the two-hour drive along Lake Superior's North Shore, a dense blanket of fog obscured the vista they usually saw when they were en route to camp on the Gunflint Trail.

The family turned inland on a logging road, deep into the valley of the Cascade. A surveyors's tag signaled their destination.

For the next two hours they had explored. They followed moose and wolf prints along the river, marveled at the scraggy spruces draped in Old Man's Beard and discovered the whitened remains of a winter kill near the river's edge. And they watched the river. It was the river that captured them. Its spirit became theirs. A few months later they worked together to build a cabin along its banks.

"Fifteen years ago," Marina thought as she climbed down from the loft, "I was still a teenager." The cabin was quiet. Marina's dad was sitting near the woodstove, keeping the fire stoked. Her mom was outside with Ben and Carolyn putting bread crumbs out for the Canadian jays. Marina walked over to the bookshelf and took out the Bunkhouse journal. Her family had decided to keep a journal to record the thoughts and events of each trip there. She opened it.

June, 1972

What a weekend! Our hammers flew as we tried to keep pace with the mosquitoes and black flies. We knocked together walls, nailed the flooring in place, cemented the chimney blocks and tarred the roof. While the rest of us picked up tools and cleared away our camping gear to prepare for the trip back to Duluth, Dad took his creel and rod down to the river. Within two hours, he was back, having caught seven brook trout—a celebration feast for six fine "carpenters" erecting a northwoods retreat.

Flipping past many years of Bunkhouse stories, Marina stopped at one of her dad's entries and began to read.

May 1, 1981

It's like starting a whole new year up here after such a lengthy absence. No sign of snow, which surprises me. The river is a little high but I'm sure I'll find some nice pockets where an unwary trout might be hooked. After breakfast, my mind and body will be prepared for a lil' trout fishing.

Marina read other entries from that spring trip. Her dad had a tradition of going to the falls to fish the first morning.

Her mom stayed behind to dig ditches, getting rid of water runoff near the cabin. Marina's dad claimed it was a childhood reversion to playing in mud and rain puddles.

Marina read on, absorbed in memories of years past. The journal recorded routines of splitting wood, feeding the jays, long conversations over the dinner table, cribbage games, hauling water from the spring and hiking to the falls and up the cliffs. She stopped at a series of entries in November of 1983. One was written by a visiting friend from Canada.

So nice to hear the hush of the river wherever you are. The Bunkhouse is a special place. You can hear all the happy hours people have spent here resounding in the trees, river and wind.

A few hours after this friend had entered his thoughts, Marina's mom and dad had come for a visit to the cabin. It was late that night. Her dad opened the journal to read what had been written, then added a few of his own thoughts.

We have descended into the Great River Basin. There is a certain feeling of survival when picking up wood in pitch darkness. As the gradual warmth from the fire penetrates the cabin, there is another

warmth. It comes from reflection upon the most tremendous children that Fran and I have conceived, the glow they instill within our hearts.

Tears welled in Marina's eyes. "This place is so much more than a retreat to the woods," she thought. "It is a retreat into each other."

The last entry described an expedition to the falls. The Bunkhouse connected three generations as Carolyn and Ben explored the river with their grandparents.

April, 1986

The trip to the falls was more of an adventure than we had planned! The trail was terribly overgrown and we had to fight the alder brush to get to the cedar forests. Carolyn crawled under the brush; Ben pushed his way through with Dad. Then we came to the cedar swamps . . . we shinnied over downed trunks and under huge, exposed roots of these ancient trees. Some of the cedars were so large that the kids and I couldn't reach around the trunk and hold hands!

The trail led through springs and pools of winter melt. Of course, Ben stepped into one and screamed as the ice-cold water seeped into his boot. Mom saved the day by donating her wool sock. We trudged on. At times we lost our way, but the sound of the river kept us true.

When we reached the glacial ridge above the old river bottom, we paused. "Listen—the low hum," said Dad to the kids. "It's the falls." The excitement in his eyes prompted Ben to take my hand. We raced to the falls as Mom and Dad helped Carolyn along. It was powerful! The water bolted over the rocks.

Marina closed the journal. Six-year-old Ben came in the cabin. "C'mon, Mom. Let's go say

'Hi' to the river," he pleaded.

"Ah, he remembers," Marina thought. The third generation was already keeping traditions alive. When all the gear was stowed away, the river had to be greeted.

Marina, her mom and the children carefully made their way down the slope. Six inches of snow covered the hand-hewn steps. The kids slid down. Marina helped her mom sidestep. Her dad was already there, deep in thought.

Perhaps he was thinking about which pockets were holding an unsuspecting trout . . . or the time he went down to the river in the early morning and saw a timber wolf cross upstream. Perhaps he was just breathing the beautiful forest air again.

"Hi, River," four-year-old Carolyn said quietly as she reached its frozen edge.

"Hi, River," Marina thought. "It's nice to be home."

Activity

Purpose To share a special natural place with those you love.

Age/Number/Setting Families—children to grandparents, other relatives and friends. A place within a two-hour drive or an hour's walk from home.

Materials Depends on your destination and how long you'll be there.

How-To Regular visits to the place will help you share its importance with others. An intimacy will develop. If it's near home, visit it daily or weekly. You can also "adopt" a campsite at a favorite park or national or state forest, or return year after year to a favorite resort.

Work together, play together. Share quiet moments around a campfire. Include children in planning, cooking and work projects. Teach kids to build fires and to fish. Watch wildlife and discover animal signs together.

Keep an open journal and photo album to record activities, seasonal changes, observations, feelings and thoughts.

Tell stories. Share what you did, saw or heard as well as ideas and feelings.

Share traditions with those who visit—a silent greeting at dawn, a daily hike, campfire building, a song or poem.

Did You Know?
Listening Points
Inspire Others

The idea of having a special place to explore and make discoveries about the earth is an old one. Children have always found such spots in the neighborhood. Families find them during vacations.

Famous naturalists have found special places. Rachel Carson purchased a cottage on the Sheepscot River near Boothbay, Maine. Conservationist Aldo Leopold turned an old chicken coop in the sand country of south-central Wisconsin into a family shack. And historic novelist of the American West, Frederic Manfred, chose the prairie hunting grounds of the Sioux to carve his stone home out of the earth. All of them believed that having a connecting point was critical to an understanding of themselves and their relationship to the earth.

Sigurd Olson found such a place on Burntside Lake in northern Minnesota. It was at the end of an old forest road, tucked away in the pines on a rock shelf. He and his wife Elizabeth sought a place that embodied the north country, but also a place they easily could reach to spend a few hours, a night or two, perhaps a week.

He called it Listening Point.

Having a connecting point was critical to an understanding of themselves and their relationship to the earth.

Each time
I have gone there
I have found . . .
the first vague
glimmerings
of meaning
in the universe.

Sigurd Olson

In a book by that title, Sigurd Olson wrote, "Each time I have gone there I have found something. . . which has opened up great realms of thought and interest . . . the first vague glimmerings of meaning in the universe, the world of knowledge and spirit."

Finding Listening Point was not easy. Olson searched the countryside near his home in Ely, Minnesota. He wanted a place to watch sunsets, moonrises and northern lights, to hear crystal clear water lapping against a little beach and a place with glaciated rocks and an area for a tent or cabin. Most of all, he wanted a vista. His vision developed from a lifetime of exploring and living in the North Country of Wisconsin and Minnesota.

"Sig" was born in Chicago, Illinois, in 1899. His family moved to northern Wisconsin by 1905. He spent his boyhood in the woods that he describes as wild country. He worked on a farm where he met his wife, Elizabeth Uhrenholdt.

When they moved to Ely, he became head of the biology department at Ely Junior College, and he began exploring the Quetico-Superior region, the Hudson Bay watershed and the Northwest Territories of Canada. For more than 20 years, he guided canoe parties during the summers.

When he returned from service in World War II, a new career awaited him. He had made the decision to share his experiences and adventures through writing.

His writing career began with adventure articles in sportsmen's magazines. Soon the emphasis in his writing changed from telling stories to sharing an affinity for the land he traveled. Olson described his style as being of a general nature with an interpretative slant aimed at increasing knowledge, awareness and appreciation of wilderness. After years of writing, editing and enduring rejections, his first book, *The Singing Wilderness*, was published in 1956. He wrote:

The singing wilderness has to do with the calling of loons, the northern lights and the great silences of a land lying northwest of Lake Superior. It is concerned with the simple joys, the timelessness and perspective found in a way of life that is close to the past.

While *The Singing Wilderness* recreated journeys in the wilderness country, *Listening Point,* his next book, described the special place he had found that exemplified the beauty of the northern landscape. Seven books followed; the last, *Of Time and Place,* was published shortly after his death in 1982. Each book shared stories of travels with family and friends in the wilderness areas throughout the Quetico-Superior. Each book shared insights and discoveries he made along the way. The opening chapter of *Listening Point* conveys the spirit of all of his books.

Listening Point is dedicated to capturing this almost forgotten sense of wonder, and learning from rocks and trees and all the life that surrounds them. Truths that can encompass all. . . . Everyone has a listening point somewhere, some quiet place to contemplate that awesome universe. This book is simply the story of what such a place has meant to me. The experiences that have been mine can be known by anyone who will make the effort.

Everyone has a listening point somewhere.

Other Ideas for Sharing Special Places

1. As a family, walk or paddle to an outlook or vista. Sit quietly together for an hour or more, sharing the rhythm and energy of the place. Share thoughts and discoveries over a cup of hot cocoa or tea when you return home. Adopt the place as a family listening point. Return to it in other seasons.

2. Pick a beach or hilltop with a beautiful view. Go there every month to watch the moon rise.

3. Find a large tree with a good place to climb and sit—an oak, pine or maple tree. Adopt "tree sitting" into your weekly routine. Bring a friend to share the view and the quiet.

4. Pick an animal that dens up in winter—a bear, a chipmunk, a raccoon, or a skunk. Find out how it burrows in for the winter. Find a good place for a den—and den up as a family. Share the warmth and fun of a family snuggle.

5. In cold weather, find the local hot spot—a hot spring, an outdoor sauna, the sunny side of trees on a snowy ridge, the southern face of a rock outcropping. Take a thermos of something warm and a reading to share with a friend or child.

6. Travel to observe a celestial event such as a solar eclipse.

7. Find out about a secret fishing hole of an elderly neighbor or grandparent. Travel there together and see if the fishing is as good as the tall tales you've been hearing.

8. Ice caves and limestone caverns are mysterious places to explore with family or friends. Mammoth Cave in Kentucky offers programs in cave exploration. Ice caves along the Great Lakes sparkle with winter's magic.

9. Find a fellow gardening enthusiast and share an experimental corner of the garden with her and your own secret methods for encouraging growth. Trade seeds and seedlings.

Resources

The Singing Wilderness by Sigurd F. Olson. New York: Alfred A. Knopf, 1956.

Listening Point by Sigurd F. Olson. New York: Alfred A. Knopf, 1958.

Open Horizons by Sigurd F. Olson. New York: Alfred A. Knopf, 1969.

A Sand County Almanac by Aldo Leopold. New York: Ballantine Books, Inc., 1970.

The House of Life: Rachel Carson at Work by Paul Brooks. Boston: Houghton-Mifflin Company, 1972.

Pilgrim at Tinker Creek by Annie Dillard. New York: Bantam Books, Inc., 1974.

Earth Festivals by Delores L. Chapelle and Janet Bourque. Silverton, CO: Finn Hill Arts, 1973.

I'm In Charge of Celebrations by Byrd Baylor. New York: Charles Scribner's Sons, 1986.

Do Not Disturb: The Mysteries of Animal Hibernation and Sleep by Margery Facklam. Boston: Little, Brown and Co., 1989.

Complete Guide to America's National Parks. New York: Viking Press, 1984-85.

Passion begins with the excitement associated with newness, such as the joy a child experiences when seeing the northern lights for the first time. It is the deep-rooted satisfaction a teenager feels when scaling a precipitous rock outcropping, secured to friends with ropes. It is the communion between friends around a blazing campfire. It is the bond between father and daughter when sharing a special place.

Passion is an embrace. It is two becoming one. Yet, in becoming one, each retains his or her uniqueness. Through passion both people grow in acceptance and love of the other.

The earth has nurtured you. By embracing the earth, you have gained insight, skills, wisdom and spiritual growth. By nurturing a sense of wonder for the earth, you have experienced curiosity and known the joys of exploring. You have discovered the rhythms and intricacies of the natural world. And you have shared those discoveries, thereby strengthening your bonds with family and friends.

But passion is more . . . far more than intense feelings. Passion extends to caring.

To sustain passion, awareness and action must follow. In a close relationship between two friends, there comes a time when each is called upon to give back, to care. When the love is strong, the only limits to caring are the limits of understanding and skill.

The feeling associated with such a profound commitment is passion. Passion develops when you are willing and able to give back. There are endless and diverse ways to give back to the earth: a child's attempt to nurture a fledgling robin; a teenager's single-handed efforts to stop a bulldozer from destroying a tract of virgin prairie; or a community's commitment to recycling its solid waste. The activities in this section of the book will help you activate your commitment and put your passion to work.

Passion, like the seasons, is an ending as well as a beginning. It is caring and being cared for. It is answering and questioning. It is giving and receiving. Passion is an embrace that leads to a commitment to love and be loved by the earth.

PASSION

15. On the Trail of John Muir

People who are committed to earth stewardship are earth prophets. They often find their entire lives transformed as they focus on visions they have for the earth—protecting an endangered species, fighting an environmental wrong or preserving a place they have come to love.

John Muir, Rachel Carson, Sigurd Olson, Aldo Leopold and others were all driven by a profound passion for the earth and its care. This passion was a unifying force in their lives. It integrated their thoughts, actions and relationships. They became prophets, not as the result of single actions or events, but because their entire lives radiated a love for the earth.

In this story we look at the life of John Muir to discover how he kept alive his sense of wonder. Muir inspired Joe to recognize his own vision of how to help preserve Fountain Lake Farm.

On the Trail of John Muir: The Story

"I've been there twice before; but I can't find it now," Joe said to himself while staring at the map. "Guess I'll just follow this road."

Joe was pursuing his fondest dream—to follow the footsteps of his favorite "earth prophet," John Muir, foster son of Wisconsin, world explorer, founder of the Sierra Club and father of the National Parks. Joe followed the unmarked winding roads that laced the wooded, sandy hills separating the Fox and Wisconsin Rivers in central Wisconsin. He was searching for Fountain Lake, Muir's boyhood home.

"It's hard to believe! Here I am, tracking one of America's most famous conservationists and almost no one around here even knows who he is, and that he spent his boyhood right here," Joe thought, staring at the map again.

According to the book, *My Boyhood and Youth*, the Muir family moved to Fountain Lake from Scotland in 1849. They named the area Fountain Lake Farm because of the farm springs that flowed into the lake. John said the lake was the source of his wonder for wildness, an inspiration for the rest of his life.

Joe stopped his car in the shade of an oak grove. He thumbed through the book and found a favorite passage about Muir's boyhood arrival at the farm.

Just as we arrived at the shanty, David and I jumped down. . . . This sudden splash into pure wildness—baptism in Nature's warm heart—how utterly happy it made us! Nature streaming into us, wooingly teaching her wonderful glowing lessons. Oh, that glorious Wisconsin wilderness!

After five years of intensive wheat farming, Fountain Lake Farm declined—its fertility extracted by the early practices of agriculture. The family then moved to "Hickory Hill" where John's father again cleared wooded hillsides and, in John's words, "mined the soil." By the early twentieth century, farmers in central Wisconsin had begun to recognize the fragile nature of the oak-hickory ecosystem. "Wilderness" was allowed to reclaim the hillsides and waterways.

Joe liked the resulting patchwork—steeper slopes were protected by oaks, and the farmers planted the valleys with small fields of corn, oats and hay.

As the car followed the winding, oak-lined road, a thunderhead approached from the west. The skies darkened. The wind began to blow. The weather reminded Joe of the different seasons and storms that Muir weathered during his years as a spokesman for wilderness—the fight to establish the great western parks of America, the battle to save the redwoods, the recognition of the Everglades. Joe had visited all of these sites and also hoped someday to visit

Glacier Bay in Alaska, a place that helped Muir solve the riddles of glaciation.

But of all the places where Joe had followed Muir's footsteps, central Wisconsin united him most firmly with Muir's sense for the bounty and beauty of nature. The Wisconsin ponds and woodlands of Muir's youth were those of Joe's own youth.

When he arrived at Fountain Lake, Joe found the sun shining brightly and ". . . the lilies and sunspangles danced together in radiant beauty." It was just as Muir had described it a hundred years earlier.

In his final years Muir reported that he continually returned to the memory of Fountain Lake. In *My Boyhood and Youth*, Muir's last book and autobiography, he wrote of the lake that gave birth to his insatiable love and passion for things and places, wild, natural and free. On its shores was molded the sense of wonder that propelled him into a life of exploration, scientific study and environmental activism. Although Muir was able to save countless mountains as national parks, his desire to preserve Fountain Lake went unrecognized.

As he approached Muir's homesite, Joe realized that changes had occurred since he was last here. A newly painted mailbox read "Fountain Lake Farm."

Along the lane leading to the house, Joe saw piles of logs and noticed the slash pushed into piles by a bulldozer. These piles of pine boughs and roots were smoldering. A slender, young man was nearby, tending one of the smoldering piles of pine boughs. His hands were blackened by the pitch and ash.

"Hi," said Joe. "I've been following the trail of John Muir and was wondering if I could see part of the old homestead. Are any of the old buildings still standing?"

"Hello," said Erik. "This is the homestead, but all of the original buildings are gone. This newer house was built in the 1900s on the same spot as the original. But if you want to look at something interesting come over and see this."

Erik gestured toward two enormous lilac bushes that overlooked the lake. John's sister, Sarah, had planted the lilacs from cuttings she brought from Scotland in 1849. They were planted on each side of their first log shanty before they built their bigger house. Sarah had been especially fond of these plantings. For her, they provided a direct tie to the old country.

Joe could hardly contain his excitement in meeting Erik. At long last he had found a kindred spirit who shared his enthusiasm about Fountain Lake!

"Not many people here realize how important Muir was," Erik said. "And those who do know about Muir don't realize how significant this lake was to him. Muir loved this place until the day he died. He said it was his baptism into wilderness. Did you know that Muir tried several times to buy back the farm so that he could protect it? Some say this was the beginning of his interest in saving areas as national parks."

"What are you trying to do here?" asked Joe. "Will you farm it like the Muirs did? Is that why you cut the trees?"

"No! No!" exclaimed Erik. "Muir himself hated the way farming destroyed the beautiful wildflowers, birds and other wildlife that abounded when they first arrived—before they cut the oaks. I think he'd like to see it more natural, so I'm cutting down the pine plantation and I hope to restore the site by planting prairie seeds and oak trees, just like it was when they arrived."

As they headed for the shade of a gigantic old maple tree, Joe asked, "How do you know the original house stood right here?"

"Well, it's been real interesting fitting the pieces of the puzzle together. First, I read everything that was written about the homeplace. But the real keys were the sketches Muir himself made of the house and of the lake while sitting on top of the old shanty. As a landscape architect, I'm very interested in historic sites and plantings. I pieced together evidence from these sketches and from old maps and aerial photographs. I also talked to the oldtimers around here and discovered that the lilacs over there were planted next to the old oak shanty."

"You have lots of plans for restoring this place. How long will all this take?" Joe asked in amazement.

"Years," Erik replied. "Getting the oaks to grow to full size will take a long time. But some of the ideas I hope to finish by next year for the 150-year anniversary of Muir's birth. So far, I've invested a lot of labor and savings into this project. I hope to get some help in reestablishing the native prairie land and labor for reconstructing some of the older buildings. Got any ideas?"

An hour quickly passed as Joe and Erik talked. They shared ideas and contacts. Would the Wisconsin Historical Society, the Sierra Club or the National Park Service be able to help? The task of restoring the homestead and organizing a 150-year commemorative event seemed monumental.

"I'm sure there are others who would be interested," said Joe. "Perhaps this is the time to approach the National Park Service. We could organize a new group, perhaps 'The John Muir Society,' to foster awareness and sponsor events for the anniversary."

"I've been thinking about that, too," said Erik. "I wrote a letter to the U.S. Postmaster General asking that a 150th-year commemorative stamp on Muir be issued. In a few weeks an elderhostel group is also coming to see Fountain Lake Farm. They might want to join in an organization we could call 'Friends of Fountain Lake Farm.' I'm hoping they will come back and help with the prairie planting."

"I can call the National Park Service," added Joe. "I think they would be interested in protecting the site. Certainly, they would want to help achieve Muir's dream of preserving Fountain Lake."

Joe looked at the sun. Time was running out, not only for the day but for this special place.

"Perhaps we could meet again in September," Joe volunteered. "There's a worldwide Congress on Wilderness in Colorado then. It would be a good time to tell others about this place. I think we could even get a Congressional resolution passed that would call for the protection of this place."

As they looked toward the lake sparkling in the breeze, Joe reflected on what the day had brought—the joy of serendipity, the power of purpose and the spirit of Muir. Joe knew he was on the trail of John Muir. Together with Erik he would follow Muir's footprints in protecting this important place. They would use Muir's own strategies—ones he had used to protect other sites.

They would contact other allies, write letters and lobby members of Congress.

As they were about to part, both realized the immense task ahead.

"Let's keep in contact," said Erik. "Let's see what we can do."

Activity

Purpose: To create a vision for the earth and pursue it.

Age/Number/Setting: This activity is designed for individual adults but can be modified for teens or families.

How-To: What dreams do you have about the outdoors? About discovering your sense of wonder? Listen to your inner voice. Identify your personal interests or concerns about the earth.

Complement quiet reflective time about this vision with reading. Read what the earth prophets have written and what they've done.

Is your vision to take extended trips as Sigurd Olson and John Muir did? To find a cottage like Rachel Carson's or an old farm, like Aldo Leopold's to restore?

Total immersion in the outdoors inspired the earth prophets to share the truths they found. Olson wrote books. Muir founded the Sierra Club. Carson's *Silent Spring* changed the course of public awareness. Leopold's land management insights dramatically changed U.S. Forest Service policies.

Articulate your vision with friends and family. Listen to their feelings about the earth. Especially listen to children and give them a sense that what they feel is important. Their visions can be so simple, so pure.

Hold your vision in your heart, even though life's tasks may sidetrack you. Nurture it through conversations, leisure reading, lectures, more time outdoors.

Finally, make a commitment. Arrange to have an entire vacation be an extended wilderness trip. Or dig up a patch of your lawn and make a big garden. Or buy that little cabin you've been dreaming about. Follow through on the vision and feel your passion grow! We can all be earth stewards if we are willing to work to make our dreams become reality.

Did You Know?
You Can Be An Earth Steward

I think of friends
who've fought
my fight
They've tumbled,
now they're gone.

Douglas Wood

The wind sends old trees crashing
A bare sky greets the dawn
I think of friends who've fought my fight
They tumbled, now they're gone.
Now who will love the land
Who will help us understand
Who will hold the sky up
Now the big trees are down?

Douglas Wood, *The EarthSong Book*, "The Big Trees are Down"

The inspiration for our book came from the earth—from listening to the whisper of wind, the songs of the night and the rush of the rivers. These pulses of nature were touchstones, the guideposts for those known as earth prophets. In this book we've referred often to several earth prophets or, as Douglas Wood calls them, "Big Trees."

John Muir, Aldo Leopold, Sigurd Olson and Rachel Carson were driven by a profound and active passion for the earth and its care. Love of nature was the unifying force in their lives. It integrated their thoughts, actions and relationships.

Many others are also worthy of being called earth prophets.

When threatened with the purchase of tribal lands by the government, Chief Seattle, of the Duwamish tribe in Washington State, sent a letter to President Pierce. He stated that the earth cannot be bought or sold. It was not Washington's to give but the Creator's. He further cautioned that, "Whatever befalls the earth befalls the sons of the earth."

Mary Hunter Austin was a champion of the southwest deserts during the early years of this century: "The secret charm of the desert is the secret of life triumphant." Her sensitivity to the land and its native people was shared in her books and her lifestyle. Austin spoke to the harmony between humankind and the earth.

Other names form a litany of caretakers—caretakers like you. As an earth caretaker, you stand as a big tree within the growing forest of environmental awareness. Listen and make your own discoveries. Share your passion for the earth with those you love.

"We"
will hold
the sky up
Now the big trees
are down.

Other Ideas for Honoring the Earth

1. Discover the origin of your own sense of wonder. Talk to parents and childhood friends, and learn what places, activities and things were important to you when you were young.

2. Select a natural or historical place that you like. Learn about its history, significance and future.

3. Visit and interview a dedicated member of a local environmental organization. In asking questions about lifestyle and vision, think about your own life and changes you can make.

4. Find out if there are any family members or neighbors with a particular interest in the environment. Contact them and find out how they got interested in the natural world.

5. Talk to your newspaper editor about running an article or series about local conservationists.

6. Talk to a local expert on forest, wetland or prairie life and learn about current restoration and preservation efforts. Volunteer to help.

7. Visit the sacred grounds of native people—the Black Hills in South Dakota, Cliff Dwellings in Arizona, Madeline Island in Lake Superior, Pipestone National Monument in Minnesota. Sense the spirit of the land. Respect the earth near your own home as sacred ground.

8. Plan a birthday party for one of the earth prophets. Gather a group of friends or your family. Share a meal, read poems or prose from their works, plan an activity in your neighborhood similar to what they worked for in their lives: Sigurd F. Olson—April 4; Rachel Carson—May 27; John Muir—April 21.

9. Make up your own "earth pledge" by which to live. Work with your children or your spouse to create a land ethic for your property.

10. Select an earth prophet or conservationist-environmentalist you would like to learn more about. Use the resources of this chapter to find stories, articles and books about your steward.

11. Describe either in a journal entry or a letter to a friend what you hope your region will look like in 50 or 100 years.

Resources

My Boyhood and Youth by John Muir. Boston: Houghton-Mifflin, 1913.

The Wilderness World of John Muir edited by Edwin Way Teale. Boston: Houghton-Mifflin, 1954.

The Life of John Muir by Linnie Marsh Wolfe. Madison: The University of Wisconsin Press, 1945.

Wilderness and the American Mind by Roderick Nash. New Haven: Yale University Press, 1967.

Wilderness Visionaries by Jim dale Vickery. Merrilville, IN: ICS Books, Inc., 1986.

The Age of Gaia: A Biography of Our Living Earth by James Lovelock. New York: W.W. Norton and Co.

For the Conservation of Earth: Proceedings of the Fourth World Wilderness Congress edited by Vance Martin. Golden, CO: Fulcrum, Inc., 1988.

Restoring the Earth: How Americans are Working to Renew our Damaged Environment by John J. Berger. New York: Alfred A. Knopf, 1986.

Landscaping for Wildlife by Minnesota Dept. of Natural Resources. 500 Lafayette Rd., Box 7, St. Paul, MN 55155, 1987.

A Garden of Wildflowers: 101 Native Species and How to Grow Them by Henry W. Art. Pownal, VT: Storey Communications Inc., 1986.

 text: PASSION

Passion
extends to
caring.

16. Bulldozers and Boardrooms

For most of us, stepping on the path to environmental activism is
not a premeditated decision. Something touches us close to home
and we feel moved to act. We may not have the skills, but we're
motivated to find help and direction because we care passionately.

The call to environmental activism is a noble cause—to do battle
for the earth, to fight to preserve it.

The battlefield may be the halls of Congress, the boardroom of a
company or the front of a bulldozer. The weapon may be a
petition, a phone call, a speech, careful research, money or even
physical force. But the battle is important. The stakes are high.

Ann once directed an effort to halt expansion of an airport in her
community. She learned how to find help and was inspired by the
example of another environmentalist.

Bulldozers and Boardrooms: The Story

The Park Point area of Duluth, Minnesota, is one of the world's longest freshwater sand bars. This narrow, four-mile-long sand spit is stabilized only by beachgrass, American beach pea and a few trees. It is an attractive residential area and in summer it is the recreational focus of this Lake Superior city.

Ann and her friends and family relish the endless sand beach. As swimmers, boaters, sunbathers and shipwatchers, they are regular summer visitors. In the winter they return to find Park Point frozen and silent—a place for those in search of solitude.

In all seasons this sand spit serves as an important barrier. It protects the Duluth-Superior shipping harbor from the rages of northeast Lake Superior storms.

"Are they really going to cut down the pine forest?" asked Ann incredulously when a fellow member of The Duluth Audubon Society explained the proposal to expand the small airport at the end of Park Point. As president of The Duluth Audubon Society, Ann had been approached by some of her fellow birdwatchers. Their feelings were unanimous. Park Point is one of the state's most scenic locations and a premier birdwatching spot. The small pine forest on the dunes provides important shelter for migrating birds.

The proposal called for the small airport on Park Point to lengthen its runway and install runway lights to meet Federal Aviation Agency safety standards. The initial plan was to clearcut an acre of pine and to destroy a small area of wetland.

The proposal went before the Duluth City Council. Ann organized an hour of testimony before the council that included herself, an ecologist, a hydrologist, birdwatchers, neighbors and other Auduboners.

The ecologist, Ann's husband Dave, told the city councilors that the vegetation on Park Point is unique. The beach and dunes are the western limit of a Great Lakes plant community and the pines are a remnant of what once stretched the entire length of the point. Dave cautioned the councilors, "This narrow forest strip is exposed to very strong winds. Cutting pines on one margin of the stand would make pines presently in the interior of the stand more vulnerable to wind damage." Auduboners strengthened their emotional plea to preserve the area's unique beauty with facts that showed how a little bit of tampering could have significant ecological effects.

Safety and money—those were the arguments brought forth by airport officials. If the changes were made, Sky Harbor Airport would meet safety standards and qualify for federal funds to make the changes. Tough arguments to refute.

Ann and her fellow Audubon members

proposed a compromise. They acknowledged the importance of safety but asked that only vegetation more than 15 feet tall be removed. This would preserve the wetland. The compromise proposal also called for limiting the removal of pines and replacing removed trees with habitat revegetation. The compromise was accepted! Construction crews came in, cut only a few pines and removed only the taller vegetation in the wetlands. Light poles were erected. The controversy settled down.

But Lake Superior had not yet written its chapter of the story. Three years after the heated city council meeting, Dave's worst predictions about tampering with the pine stand came true. A severe June storm blew down many pines that had been weakened by the cutting of trees next to the runway. If the initial clear-cutting proposal had been followed, the entire pine stand probably would have blown down in one storm, leaving the airport totally at the mercy of Lake Superior.

Ann and Dave walked along the beach to examine the damage. They were shocked to see dozens of 100-foot pines lying in disarray as if victims of some monstrous game of pick-up sticks. Searching for some evidence of the habitat revegetation efforts, the pair walked over to the light poles. A few barren, knee-high shrubs were scattered here and there—a token effort at best.

"This really makes me angry," Ann said to Dave. "The airport authority has not carried out their part of the compromise in good faith." So, three years later she reluctantly re-entered the battle to preserve her beloved Park Point.

Ann used the storm's damage as leverage to remind the airport authority that it had still not done the extensive replanting that had been promised. A letter to the editor of the newspaper and a phone call to the airport authority prompted the hiring of a landscaper who worked with Dave to come up with a plan for replanting.

Meanwhile, a larger issue remained. What if another airport expansion proposal were to threaten more of the land at the end of the sand spit? That was the question the Duluth Audubon Conservation Committee had worried about since the compromise agreement had been struck with the city council.

During the next three years the committee worked with state officials to forge a proposal to designate the end of Park Point as a scientific and natural area. Local officials balked at this restrictive classification. They refused the state's offer. Because there was no immediate threat of expansion, the Audubon committee decided to move on to other issues. Ann, too, was tempted to let go of the concern about future problems. But then she heard a story that changed her attitude.

Ann had been working with Peg Kohring, director of the Minnesota chapter of The Nature Conservancy. Ann was to write a story about a small prairie tract in southern Minnesota. Peg, a botanist by heart and by training, shared with Ann a story about how she once had to fight to save a tract of prairie.

"I never intended to be an activist," said Peg. "But when I was 18, I was out collecting seeds for a nature center and I came upon a bulldozer

operator destroying one of my collecting sites."
She described jumping up and down to attract
the attention of the operator. "He just waved
politely. That simply made me angrier. So, I
walked closer to the bulldozer and began talking
loudly. The operator was curious enough to
bring the machine to a halt."

The skinny, blonde teenager told the 'dozer
operator, "This is pure virgin prairie. You can't
bulldoze it." The operator was amused.

She persisted, "If you'll come into town and
have a cup of coffee with me, I'll tell you why
you shouldn't bulldoze this stretch of prairie."
The operator finished the stretch he was working on, then accompanied her to the cafe.

Peg explained in great detail the importance
of prairies. He concluded, "Well, it's not my
decision, lady. You gotta call the district engineer."

An hour later, Peg strode into the boardroom
of the Amtrak district engineer's office. "What
are you doing bulldozing that tract of prairie?"
she demanded.

"What are you doing trespassing on our
property?" countered the man with the huge
handlebar mustache and a twinkle in his blue
eyes. He laughed at the crusader in front of him,
but agreed to accompany her to look at the
prairie tract.

After a day in the field, Peg had convinced
the engineer that some of the areas he was
clearing were valuable prairie tracts. He, in turn,
had convinced Peg of the importance of cutting
brush to give a clear field of vision to the train
operators. Together they agreed to protect four

tracts with unique prairie habitat. The Amtrak
official would see that they were not bulldozed,
and Peg agreed to handcut the brush. The compromise pleased them both, although for Peg it
meant hours and hours of laborious hand-cut-
ting. Eventually she got the prairie tracts established as natural areas of The Nature
Conservancy and this fourth-generation
botanist became the youngest person ever to
direct a Midwest Nature Conservancy state office.

"If Peg can handcut brush to protect a prairie,
then surely I can keep plugging away at the
paperwork it's going to take to permanently
protect Park Point," thought Ann. And so, four
years after that first heated city council debate,
she decided to begin a letter-writing campaign.

Since that decision, Ann has written a dozen
letters attempting to get Park Point included in
national legislation designed to protect all un-
developed coastal barrier areas. She has her congressional representative on her side. The
national environmental coalition working on
this issue is well aware of Park Point. But after
seven years of battling to preserve the quality of
natural beauty on her sand bar, Ann is far from
predicting long-term success.

Yet, each time Ann launches her sea kayak off
the smooth sand into Lake Superior's inviting
surf she is reminded that Park Point is a treasure.
And each time she swims or builds sand castles
with her children on the Point, she reaffirms
that the future is important and that she can
help shape it. So, she keeps agitating for permanent protection of Park Point.

Activity

Purpose
To fight for an environmental concern.

Age/Number/Setting
There's no limit. Your fight might be over a local issue; it might be statewide or even global in scale.

Materials
A telephone, letter-writing materials, transportation, maybe the FAX machine at your nearest copying center.

How-To
Choose an environmental issue that gets your blood boiling.

Talk to experts who have information that will help you define the problem: scientists, agriculture extension personnel, state and federal land managers, engineers. What are the benefits and values threatened? Who are the key people?

Go directly to the developer or city official responsible for the problem. Seek allies that will help you express your concern. See "Did You Know?" for helpful hints on finding an ally.

Talk to elected officials who have jurisdiction over the problem you seek to address. Elected officials do respond to calls from their constituents.

If you feel that a phone call is not enough, arrange for a personal visit. Remember that an elected official may be more likely to take the time to meet with you if you arrange to have several other concerned citizens present.

Determine your course of action. You may need to: file a complaint, demand a public hearing, get a newspaper reporter to do an article, write a letter to the editor of the newspaper, establish your own group or testify at a public hearing.

If you choose to write elected officials, here are some pointers:

- Use personal or business letterhead and include your full return address on both the letter and the envelope.

- Clearly identify your issue. Stick to one subject per letter. If you are lobbying on behalf of some legislation, give the name and number of the House or Senate bill.

- State your reason for writing. Express your feelings. Explain in your own words how the issue in question affects you and why your representative or senators should be concerned.

- Be brief. A letter of 50 or 100 words is easiest to write and to read.

- Ask your representative or senator to state his or her position in response. Remember that your elected officials work for you.

- Take the time to thank them for their assistance.

Finally, follow through. One phone call to an official is not enough. One letter to a developer is not enough. Your letter can too easily be filed. Persistence is the key to success, and you are responsible for that persistence.

Did You Know?
Others Care, Too

In the story, Peg Kohring went directly to the developer with her concerns. That approach takes a lot of self confidence. Most people seek the support of an environmental group to help them fight earth issues.

Local chapters of organizations like the the Sierra Club, The National Audubon Society or the Izaak Walton League are a good place to begin. National environmental organizations have expertise to offer their local chapters. They have lobbyists at work in Washington, D.C., and in many state capitols. They know how local violations of national laws like the Clear Water Act can be fought. And they have the staff and resources to help. Most have a contact number listed in the phone book.

Local environmental groups with names like Cedar Valley Conservation Club or Douglas County Conservation Society or Protectors of the Allegheny can be especially helpful. They may not have national lobbying ties, but they have insight into local political personalities and mechanisms. And although they may not be listed in the phone book, their names and contact people can be found simply by talking with local officials or informed friends.

It is estimated that 25 million people in the U.S. may be involved in one way or another, in local and regional conservation issues ranging from groundwater contamination to wildlife preservation.

How do you select an environmental group to join? If it is a local group or a national group with a local chapter, the best way to find out if the group fits you is to attend meetings. Talk to other members and find out what kind of projects they have been

Seek the support of an environmental group to help you fight earth issues.

Environmental
groups have begun
to work
together.

involved with. If you decide to affiliate with a national group, write for their descriptive literature.

In 1985 the "Big 10" of the environmental movement worked together to outline a much-debated Environmental Agenda for the Future. The "Big 10" included: Environmental Defense Fund, Environmental Policy Institute, Friends of the Earth, Izaak Walton League of America, Natural Resources Defense Council, The National Audubon Society, National Parks and Conservation Association, National Wildlife Federation, the Sierra Club and The Wilderness Society.

However, those 10 organizations are by no means an exhaustive list of effective national environmental organizations. Earth First! and the Sea Shepherd Conservation Society of Los Angeles are more radical national groups that are committed to environmental sabotage as a means of change.

Greenpeace, one of the first international environmental organizations, now has nearly one million members. In the last few years other international groups have added their voices of concern for the survival of our planet. They include Worldwatch Institute, World Resources Institute, the Better World Society and the Global Tomorrow Coalition.

It is also important to note that in recent years many environmental organizations have begun to work together. In 1988 environmental organizations created a "Blueprint for the Environment" and delivered it to President George Bush. Many environmental organizations also worked together on the 1989 Alaskan oil spill.

Other Ideas for Environmental Activism

1. Sponsor a neighborhood or park cleanup. Do it as part of a spring and fall cleaning schedule.

2. Support the work of national environmental groups by joining The Wilderness Society, Greenpeace, Earth First, The National Audubon Society, the Sierra Club or another national organization. Check out local conservation groups and consider joining a committee.

3. Set up an environmental kids club such as "Kids for the Earth." Organize a neighborhood litter patrol. Design your own badge.

4. Set up a coffee clutch with two or more friends to discuss an environmental book. A good one to start with is *50 Simple Things You Can Do to Save the Earth.*

5. Adopt a whale through the Whale Adoption Project, 634 North Falmouth Highway, PO Box 388, North Falmouth, MA 02556.

6. Join a Volunteer in the Park program. Contact a city, county, state or national park for information.

7. Become a junior naturalist through a city, county or state park program. Or earn your nature badge in a scouting program.

8. When you see signs of pollution, contact an official and ask for help tracing it to the source.

9. Organize a park appreciation day.

10. Attend a public hearing on an environmental issue. Take your children along with you.

11. Volunteer to work a day at a recycling center. Or set up a recycling option for people at a local picnic, sporting event or concert.

12. Organize a protest of an event or proposed development that may be harmful to the environment.

Resources

An Environmental Agenda for the Future edited by Robert Cahn. Washington, DC: Island Press, 1985.

The State of the World: 1989: A World-Watch Institute Report on Progress Towards a Sustainable Society. W.W. Norton and Company, 1989.

Blueprint for the Environment: A Plan for Federal Action edited by T. Allan Camp. Howe Brothers, 1989.

Crossroads: Environmental Priorities for the Future edited by Peter Borrelli. Washington, DC: Island Press, 1988.

The Rights of Nature: A History of Environmental Ethics by Roderick Nash. Madison, WI: University of Wisconsin Press, 1989.

Design with Nature by Ian McHarg. Garden City, NJ: Doubleday & Co., Inc., 1971.

The Endangered Kingdom: The Struggle to Save America's Wildlife by Roger DiSilvestro. John Wiley and Sons, Inc., 1989.

The Conservation Directory 1990: A List of Organizations, Agencies, and Officials Concerned with Natural Resource Use and Management. Washington, DC: National Wildlife Federation, 1990.

1990 Annual Environmental Sourcebook: 159 Books for Better Conservation and Management available from Island Press, 1718 Connecticut Ave. N.W., Suite 300, Washington, DC 20009.

The Nature Conservancy Magazine. A periodical of The Nature Conservancy, 1815 North Lynn Street, Arlington, VA 22209.

PASSION

Passion
extends to
caring.

17. Wisdom's Ways

By living closer to the land, you and the earth begin to live
together like loved ones. You notice the subtle changes of gray in a
November forest, the delicate tracks marking a winter landscape,
the burgeoning pulse of life in a marigold marsh, the blessing of a
sprouting bean. You care about changes on the earth and you vow
to live gently with it.

Living gently happens in cities and in rural townships around the
world when people turn off lights, conserve water, use public
transportation, recycle or grow chemical-free gardens. In the
following story a young married couple seeks the advice and
friendship of elderly neighbors about how to begin a simpler,
more earth-conscious lifestyle.

167

Wisdom's Ways: The Story

Marina and David sat on the radiator.

"Now lean your back against that pipe," David instructed.

"Is this a joke?" asked Marina, looking for that special gleam in her friend's 72-year-old eyes.

"No, no, I'm dead serious. That's the best place to sit in this whole house."

She leaned back cautiously, then felt the warmth caress every vertebrae. He noted her pleasure.

"You know, David, I really like winter," Marina sighed. "I wish I could stay home all the time just to linger with moments like this."

David laughed. "You're absolutely right. If I've said it once, I've said it a thousand times. The best thing about wood heat is that it's the perfect excuse to stay at home and relax with Old Man Winter."

They both chuckled. Outside of World War II, David hadn't ever set foot outside of Bayfield County, Wisconsin. Marina, however, had strayed from where she was born. She had moved 70 miles east from northern Minnesota to northern Wisconsin. David forgave her. He sensed a kindred spirit.

Just then David's wife of 30 years stepped out of the kitchen with supper.

"Holly, you're a charmer," said David tenderly. "Look at this feast you've prepared!"

It was a fine meal, too. Everything was homegrown—potatoes, peas and carrots from their garden that summer; Lake Superior whitefish his brother Harvey had caught that morning, and . . .

"Where's the biscuits?" frowned David.

"Stop your fretting, David," said Holly. "I wouldn't forget. Grant is just taking them out of the cookstove."

"Don't forget the maple syrup for those biscuits," David called to Marina's husband.

Every spring for the past 50 years, David and Holly had made their own maple syrup. These days, Grant and Marina and other friends helped David and Holly in their 40-acre sugarbush on a ridge overlooking Lake Superior.

Their sugarshack where they boiled down the sap was a cedar log cabin David had built in 1936. He and Holly spent the first few years of their married life living in it.

Bowed heads. Thankful stomachs. Inner warmth. As the tea was poured, conversation picked up.

"Tell me about the cabin you're going to build," David said to Grant.

"It'll be eight-sided and solar heated," Grant began. Grant dreamed about building a traditional log house, but adapting it to use passive solar energy and earth sheltering.

"Oh, Lordy, how you gonna notch it?" asked David.

"We'll V-notch it using a double-level scribe. Should fit so tight we won't have to chink it," Grant replied.

"How about the windows?" David continued. "Did I explain to you about notching two-by-fours in the logs before you put the window in? It'll help when the house settles." Grant and Marina listened intently. David had built a few log cabins in his day. They sensed there were many tricks of the trade to learn.

David and Holly seemed to love everything they did, whether it was maple syruping or dyeing yarn with onion skins and marigolds. Both had grown up with a pioneer spirit—hardworking, honest, up-at-dawn, to-bed-after-dark. Holly was born among the wheat fields of western Minnesota and also lived in the prairies of North Dakota. David's family moved to Bayfield in 1856. An East Coast doctor told his grandfather to seek "pine-and-balsam-scented air for his consumption."

"We've dabbled in pretty nearly everything that a body can dabble in," said David proudly. "We've sold land, cut timber, done commercial and sport fishing, rented cottages and operated a truck garden that produced fruit and vegetables for the logging camps across Northern Wisconsin. My father was the strawberry king of Wisconsin for several years. We shipped one-and-a-half carloads a day by train during the height of the berry season."

During the berry season, in the middle of June, David and Grant had gone out to pick strawberries for their dessert. The berry patch was covered with netting so the birds wouldn't get to the berries first.

"Did you ever see finer berries?" David would always ask.

The plants were hilled up, with healthy runners ready to be cut and planted for next year's crop. The patch was weedless and freshly hoed. They plucked only the ripest berries.

"That's the key to good eats," David told Grant. "Let the others ripen."

Grant just listened, waiting for his chance, in a few years, once his cabin was built, to try out David's wizardry on his own homestead.

Sometimes it seemed like they raced through dinner, so eager were they for the strawberry ritual. Once the ingredients were brought in, all eyes were trained on David for instruction.

"Before we begin, I'd just like to say what a privilege it is for Holly and me to be with you young folks. We're truly blessed."

Marina bowed her head. "No, we're the ones who are blessed," she thought.

"Now, remember," David began. "The person who can match my portion of strawberry shortcake bite-for-bite wins a quart of strawberries. And remember, don't be stingy with the ice cream on top. Why, when I was a boy the first thing I did in the morning was crank three gallons for dinner. I reckon I have eaten more ice cream than anyone my age. I'm sure of it!"

As Grant and Marina stepped out the door to go home that night, David slipped Grant a quart of strawberries. "Not too bad for a young'un," David chuckled as he patted Grant on the back.

Activity

Purpose To develop a lifestyle based on a passionate caring for the earth by visiting someone who can teach you the skills.

Age/Number/Setting Although this activity can be accomplished alone, groups of children, families or friends lend support and encouragement. Small children need an adult's guidance for consistency. The activity can occur anyplace—home, school or at work.

Materials Varies with the aspect of environmental lifestyle being examined: food production, energy consumption or transportation.

How-To Changing one's lifestyle is a reflection of a love for the earth. Think about what you can do to make the world more beautiful —consume less, plant trees or flowers, reuse or recycle, heal an injury to the earth.

Find a lifestyle issue that is important to you—living in an energy-efficient home, producing some of your own food, recycling, investing money in earth-conservation organizations. Pick one area that affects you every day and work on it.

Talk about your plans with someone—a neighbor, workers at a food cooperative or power companies, professionals with environmental organizations or with university extension services. How does your present lifestyle affect the earth? Are there other ways to live? See "Did You Know?" and "Resources" for suggestions and references.

For permanent change to take place, consistency is important. Begin slowly with a lifestyle change here and there. Keep asking questions and learning new skills or techniques that promote the change you wish to make.

Did You Know?
The Earth Needs Your Help

The United States contains six percent of the world's population, yet consumes 40 percent of its resources. The result of America's use of non-renewable resources, as well as its "throw-away" attitude toward other materials, threatens the earth's ability to sustain a healthy environment.

Groundwater supplies one out of every two U.S. families with drinking water. Since 1980, there has been a 12 percent increase in use. Cities in California are seeking water from Canada. At least one-third of our country's underground storage tanks are leaking motor fuels and chemical solvents into this precious resource.

Seventy-five percent of the lakes in New Hampshire and Rhode Island and 43 percent of the lakes in the Upper Midwest are being seriously damaged by acid deposition.

Increasing amounts of particulates and dioxides have been measured in the nation's air. As more wood and fossil fuels (oil, gas, coal) are burned, releasing carbon dioxide into the atmosphere, a global warming or "greenhouse effect" occurs.

World energy demand is expected to increase 58 percent by the year 2000. Nuclear sources will proliferate to meet the demand. Oil, natural gas and coal are being depleted, but money for research and development of alternative energies (solar, wind, geothermal and hydro) continues to be cut back.

Disposal of solid waste continues to be a problem. Overpackaging, unnecessary use of non-biodegradable materials and hazardous wastes (seven billion tons a year) contribute to this problem.

The United States contains 6 percent of the world's population, yet consumes 40 percent of its resources.

We travel together, passengers on a little spaceship.

Departments of natural resources in Minnesota and Wisconsin have issued health advisories about eating fish from inland lakes.

The space program provided a catalyst for understanding the earth's plight. While orbiting the earth, astronauts turned their eyes homeward to see a beautiful blue and white ball spinning in the blackness of space. The fragility of its existence struck them. In 1970, before the United Nations General Assembly, Ambassador Adlai Stevenson turned that vision into a challenge:

> We travel together, passengers on a little spaceship, dependent on its vulnerable resources of air and soil, all committed for our safety to its security and peace; preserved from annihilation only by the care, the work, and I will say, the love we give our fragile craft.

What can one individual do? How can one person affect the deterioration of the ozone layer, acid deposition or diminishing groundwater supplies? The answer is simple: consume less. Each of us uses the earth's resources; each of us can conserve them.

Lester R. Brown, President of World Watch Institute, looks to the simplification of lifestyles to reconcile the needs of the person, the community, the economy and the environment.

What is an environmental lifestyle?

It requires *conserving* human and material resources (food, fuel, water, wildlife): Use only those materials essential to basic human needs of food, shelter and clothing. Buy durable items made from renewable resources. Recycle, reuse or repair products rather than discard them.

An environmental lifestyle begins with *educating* yourself and others about the care of the earth. Keep informed about pollution and support action that alleviates such problems. Teach environmentally-sound concepts of living to your family.

An environmental lifestyle is *advocating* a perspective of change:
Question the social myths of growth, progress and development.
Try to live life at a slower pace. Take time to appreciate the people
and other living beings that you interact with each day.

Adopting an environmental lifestyle means making physical and
attitudinal changes in the way you live. The changes will be
determined by who you are, where you live, and what you do for a
living—and by your own imagination and ingenuity.

Other Ideas for Living Gently

1. Contact the local power company to conduct an energy audit of your home, school or workplace. Research how you could reduce energy use and consumption. Assign priorities to the items on your list of projects, and get to work!

2. Work with family members, teachers or fellow workers to establish a conservation award-of-the-week or month.

3. Focus on your garden. Find ways to make it more organic. For example, explore the option of companion planting (certain plants need certain other plants to stimulate their growth) and using organic nutrients from a compost pile to add to the soil.

4. Plant a tree for a special event and assume long-term responsibility for its care.

5. Plant an edible landscape for yourself, the birds and the squirrels. Rose bushes, nut and fruit trees, berry plants, honeysuckle and grape vines will be enjoyed by all.

6. Set aside part of your yard, or a neighborhood plot, to produce some of your own food. Involve children in sprouting seeds, transplanting seedlings and watering the plants. Plan a harvest dinner with your bounty.

7. Recycle your wastes. Compost kitchen wastes for use in gardens. Use both sides of your writing paper. Encourage city councils to pass a recycling ordinance—to accept glass, newsprint, cardboard, metal and aluminum cans. Don't buy items that have excessive packaging.

8. Walk to school or work. Use public transportation or a carpool.

9. With a child or friend, respond thoughtfully and carefully to the needs of an injured plant or animal. Provide food, shelter and rest. Seek a vet if needed. The desire to heal a wounded creature comes naturally and makes a powerful contribution to the earth at large.

10. Celebrate earth holidays: Earth Day is April 22; equinoxes usually fall on September 23 and March 21, solstices on June 21 and December 21. Prepare stories, sing songs, dance and make special meals. Think of a gift to give to the earth.

Resources

Green Lifestyle Handbook: 1001 Ways You Can Heal the Earth edited by Jeremy Rifkin. New York: Henry Holt and Co., 1990.

50 Things You Can Do to Save the Earth by The Earthworks Group. Berkeley, CA: Earthworks Press, 1990.

Voluntary Simplicity by Duane Elgin. New York: William Morrow and Company, Inc., 1981.

99 Ways to a Simple Lifestyle edited by Albert J. Fritschm. Garden City: Anchor Books, 1976.

Small is Beautiful: Ecomonics as if People Mattered by E.F. Schumacher. New York: Harper and Row, 1973.

Economics as if the Earth Really Mattered: A Catalyst Guide to Socially Conscious Investing by Lowry Meeker. Santa Cruz, CA: New Society Publishers, 1988.

The Integral Urban House: Self-Reliant Living in the City by Farallones Institute. San Francisco: Sierra Club Press, 1979.

Diet for a Small Planet by Frances Moore Lappe. New York: Ballantine Books, 1974.

Chop Wood, Carry Water: A Guide to Finding Spiritual Fulfillment in Everyday Life by Rick Fields, and editors of New Age Journal. Los Angeles: Jeremy P. Tarcher, Inc., 1984.

Wellness Workbook by John Travis and Regina Ryan. Berkeley, CA: Ten Speed Press, 1988.

The Spirit of the Earth: A Theology of the Land by John Hart. Ramsey, NJ: Paulist Press, 1984.

A Spirituality Named Compassion: The Healing of the Global Village by Matthew Fox. New York: Harper and Row, 1979.

GAIA: An Atlas of Planet Management edited by Dr. Norman Myers. Garden City: Anchor Press, 1984.

Magazines:

The Mother Earth News
P.O. Box 70
Hendersonville, NC 28791

Creation
Matthew Fox, Editor
160 E. Virginia St. #280
San Jose, CA 95112

Utne Reader
2732 W. 43rd Street
Minneapolis, MN 55410

Environmental Action
1525 New Hampshire Ave. NW
Washington, D.C. 20036

Positive Vibrations
P.O. Box 593, Station E
Victoria, British Columbia
V8W256

World Watch
World Watch Institute
776 Massachusetts Ave. NW
Washington, D.C. 20036

The Environmental Magazine
P.O. Box 6667
Syracuse, NY 13217

Harrowsmith Country Life
The Creamery
Charlotte, VT 05445